D1480409

INUIT MYTHOLOGY

Evelyn Wolfson

Enslow Publishers, Inc.

40 Industrial Road	PO Box 38
Box 398	Aldershot
Berkeley Heights, NJ 07922	Hants GU12 6BP
USA	UK

http://www.enslow.com

I thank Dorothy Tweer and Dacia Callen Wolfson
for their advice, criticism, and comments.

Library of Congress Cataloging-in-Publication Data

Wolfson, Evelyn.
    Inuit mythology / Evelyn Wolfson.
        p. cm. – (Mythology)
    Includes bibliographical references and index.
    ISBN 0-7660-1559-9
    1. Inuit mythology—Juvenile literature. [1. Inuit—Folklore. 2. Eskimos—
Folklore. 3. Folklore—Arctic regions.] I. Title. II. Series: Mythology (Berkeley
Heights, N.J.)
    E99.E7 W78 2001
    398.2'089'9712—dc21   00-055146

Printed in the United States of America

10 9 8 7 6 5 4 3 2 1

To Our Readers:
We have done our best to make sure all Internet addresses in this book were
active and appropriate when we went to press. However, the author and the
publisher have no control over and assume no liability for the material available
on those Internet sites or on other Web sites they may link to. Any comments or
suggestions can be sent by e-mail to comments@enslow.com or to the address
on the back cover.

Cover and Illustrations by William Sauts Bock

CONTENTS

Map 4

Preface 6

1 *The Woman Who Adopted a Bear*
Polar Inuit of Northern Greenland 21

2 *The Girl Who Married a Gnome*
Inuit of West and East Greenland 42

3 *The Adventures of Kivioq*
Netsilik of Nunavut, Canada 55

4 *Sedna, Goddess of the Sea*
Baffinland Inuit of Nunavut, Canada . . . 67

5 *Oogoon's Adventures on
the Kobuk River*
The Inuit of Kotzebue Sound, Alaska . . . 78

6 *The Hill Giant*
Bering Strait Inuit of Alaska 94

7 *Ol-an-uk the Orphan*
Aleuts, or Unangan, of Alaska 106

Glossary 119

Chapter Notes 121

Further Reading 125

Internet Addresses 126

Index 127

Arcti

Russia

China ←

Siberia

Beaufort S

Cape
Espenberg

Aleutian-Trench

Bering Strait

Kotzebue Sound

KOTZEBUE

Cape
Thomp

ALEUT

Bering Sea

Seward Peninsula

Norton Sound

Alaska

N

Bering

ALEUTIAN ISLANDS

Ca

(UNANGAN)

Gulf
of Alaska

Japan

Current

Canada

Pacific Ocean

Summer tent   Igloo   wooden house

Map of Inuit
territory

KAYAK   UMIAK

ean
rth
e
Iceland
Denmark Strait
E. GREENLAND INUIT
Greenland
POLAR INUIT
W. GREENLAND INUIT
Europe →
Baffin Bay
Davis Strait
Bellot strait
Baffin Island
Gulf of Boothia
Labrador Sea
Victoria Strait
NETSILIK
Committee Bay
INUIT
NUNAVUT
Hudson Bay
Canada
dian - Arctic
N
E
S
ted States
Atlantic Ocean

 PREFACE

The homeland of the Inuit (IN-oo-aht) people is a broad region of frozen land and sea that stretches from Alaska in the west to Greenland in the east. It is a land where trees are unable to grow, and only the hardiest animals and people can survive. Today, people of the North American Arctic are called Inuit, a term that has replaced the word *Eskimo*. Few of today's modern Inuit live where their parents or grandparents were born. Instead, they live in small cities and towns, mostly in southern regions of the Arctic. Traditional houses have been replaced by imported wooden ones, dogsleds have been replaced by snowmobiles, oil lamps have been replaced by electric lights and central heat, most foodstuffs must be imported, and television is the most important source of entertainment.

The Arctic covers the northernmost part of the earth and includes three continents: North America, Asia, and Europe. Less than one third of the Arctic is land. The rest is covered by the Arctic Ocean. The Inuit have lived in the North American Arctic for thousands of years. Descended from an early Siberian people, the Inuit arrived later to the New World than Native Americans. After they crossed the Bering Strait, they settled in Arctic North America and developed their own unique culture. Earlier and different groups of emigrants who came from Siberia and China beginning twenty-five to thirty thousand years ago migrated into the interior of North America and southward along the coast to South America.[1]

Due to the tilt of the earth's axis above the Arctic Circle, the sun's rays never shine directly down onto the earth's surface, and only a few inches of snow melt each year, leaving a foundation of permafrost, or land that never melts. In the southern Arctic, winter takes up six months of the year; and spring, summer, and fall fill the remaining months. From November until January the sun remains below the horizon, cloaking the frozen land and sea of the Arctic in total darkness. Most regions of the Arctic experience extremely cold temperatures in winter, and in January temperatures often average between 30 degrees below zero to 15 degrees below zero (Fahrenheit). As one travels northward, winter takes up more and more of the year, until, in the most northerly regions of the Arctic, winter lasts nine long months—from September until June.

Over a period of several thousand years, the Inuit spread westward across the frozen tundra, a treeless stretch of frozen land that began where the northern forest ended and extended to the Arctic Circle. The people traveled from Alaska to Greenland following the rhythm of the seasons, always in search of food. In winter and spring they hunted seals, whales, and walruses; in summer and fall they fished and hunted caribou; and all year round they sought polar bears and musk ox. The Inuit adapted well to the severely limited resources of the region and met all their everyday needs using only the animals they hunted, the rocks that lined the shores, a limited supply of plants, and a precious offering of driftwood that washed in from the sea.

Religion and Mythology

At the time of European contact, in the 1500s, the Inuit people shared basic religious beliefs and exploited the same natural resources. Life was a constant struggle for survival, and the threat of starvation was ever-present. The idea of a God, or a group of gods, to be worshiped was altogether alien to the Inuit. The Inuit believed that it was the powerful forces of nature that affected their lives. It was these forces that focused on balancing mankind's needs with those of the rest of the world.[2]

In Greenland and Canada, the Inuit had no real creation myth. In Alaska, Raven was creator. Raven stories from Alaska resemble Native American Raven stories from the Northwest Coast. In Canada and Greenland there were a few simple myths about how the world was created but no myths that resembled the Raven tales. A Netsilik woman from Canada expressed her view of creation to Knud Rasmussen, the Danish explorer, in one sentence: "The earth was as it is at the time when our people began to remember."[3]

Unlike American Indians, the Inuit of Greenland and Canada did not have a mythological time period that took place before the appearance of humans during which animals behaved like people; thus mythological stories were scarce. However, one myth, the story about Sedna, the mother of all sea animals, was so widely distributed and had so many versions throughout Canada and Greenland that it made up for the otherwise lacking store of mythological tales.

Another lesser Greenland/Canada story was told about the origin of the sun and moon. It was about two siblings who argued and then chased each other out of their house carrying torches. The girl carried a brightly lit torch, but the brother's torch was dimly lit. The sister and brother rose up into the sky, and she became sun and he moon.

Unlike the mythologies of American Indians, in stories throughout the Arctic there was little mention of a transformer, or a character empowered to change people's forms. And the only trickster, or culture hero, was Raven in Alaska.

The Inuit believed that all living beings had a soul that defined their strength and character as well as their appearance. After people died, their souls went up to join the stars and then became spirits. After animals died, their spirits went to live in a new generation of their species.

The Inuit observed important rules in their daily life to insure the well-being of the spirits. Many taboos, or bans, were associated with hunting and with caring for the bodies of dead animals. The Inuit conducted ceremonies and rituals to honor the spirits and observed important taboos to insure their good will. Taboos prohibited people from behaving in a way that would bring bad luck. For example, animal meat that had been taken on land could not be eaten or stored with meat that had been taken from the sea. Women could not sew new cloth or repair old garments after the spring sealing season ended. Instead, they would have to wait until the end of the caribou season in fall. In addition, certain rituals had to be carried out prior to butchering an animal. Before a seal could be butchered, for instance, its carcass was brought indoors and a lump of snow was dipped in water and dripped into the seal's mouth to quench the thirst of its soul.[4]

The Inuit world was filled with powerful spirits capable of vengeful and hostile acts toward people. But ordinary people could speak to the spirits and ask for help by using magical words. Magical words were kept very private and would lose their power if spoken in the presence of another person. People would also wear a magical charm, or amulet, in the form of a piece of fur sewn to clothing, or an animal tooth, claw, or bone worn as a necklace or on a belt. Amulets held spirit power and gave the wearer the character and strength of the animal whose object he or she was wearing.

When people could not appease angry spirits on their own, they sought help from an *angatok*, or shaman. Shamans had very strong contact with spirits and could see things that were not visible to ordinary men. They had the power to control ghosts and evil spirits and could cure illness, end bad weather, and bring animals back to life. When Danish explorer Knud Rasmussen asked an old shaman about his view of life, the old man responded, "Privation and suffering are the only things that can open the mind of man to those things which are hidden to others."[5]

Food, Clothing, Shelter, and Transportation

The Inuit lived in winter houses for part of the year and summer houses the rest of the year. In Greenland and Canada, the Inuit lived in igloos, or snow houses, built out on the frozen sea ice during the winter. Or, they lived in winter stone houses built on land. The Inuit of Alaska lived most of the year in houses partially dug into the ground.

Throughout the Arctic, house interiors featured wooden or stone platforms raised above the ground. The platforms ran along one wall and created a place for sitting that elevated the family off the cold ground. Thick sealskin or caribou hides covered the platforms, and each family's space on the bench was marked by a cooking lamp. Outside the house, meat was kept in separate sheds, or on tall driftwood storage racks built high above the ground and away from hungry animals. A family might consist of a mother and father and one or two children, or it might include grandparents and unmarried brothers and sisters. After a couple was married, they went to live with the man's parents because it was important for men to remain close to their family's hunting grounds.

Throughout the Arctic, the Inuit built simple summer shelters that were framed with driftwood or whalebone and covered with sealskins or caribou skins.

Men hunted seals in kayaks, a type of long, narrow single-man boat. They used whalebone or driftwood as a frame for the boat and covered the frame with sealskins. Families and supplies were transported in umiaks, large rounded boats similarly framed but covered with walrus skins.

Dogsleds carried supplies, and sometimes small children or the elderly, across the frozen land and sea. Dogsleds were made with whalebone runners and caribou-hide seats. Few families owned more than one or two sled dogs. They could not afford to feed the animals needed to pull the sleds. Often they had no dogs at all. In that case, men and women did the pulling.

Throughout the Arctic the Inuit made use of bone, antler, and the tusks of walrus and musk ox, which they carved into darts, harpoons, and spears. Inuit women carved the centers out of blocks of soft stone, called soapstone, to make durable cooking pots, bowls, and containers. Blubber, the layer of fat beneath the skins of seals and walruses, was used as fuel oil in soapstone lamps. Because blubber-fueled lamps did not give off smoke while burning, these lamps worked well indoors for cooking, heating, and lighting.

Clothing made from seal intestines was lightweight and waterproof. But the warmest clothing, usually *anoraks* (parkas) and pants, were made from caribou fur, an excellent insulating material because the hair, or fur of the animal, is hollow. Warm durable boots were made from sealskins. Bird bones made excellent sewing needles, and sinew, the long thin tendons of caribou, was used as thread.

Inuit men and women were indispensable to each other, and teamwork in marriage was essential for survival. Men did the hunting, and women did the cooking, scraping and sewing of animal hides, and provided the childcare. Because the survival of a family or community depended on male hunters, female children were not considered as valuable as male children and were often killed shortly after birth. For this reason, the number of males outnumbered that of females in the Arctic, and mature women were in great demand. The struggle to obtain a wife was a constant one, and a man would sometimes kill another man to take his wife. Women were often traded, abducted, or exchanged, and their desires and feelings were largely ignored.

The responsibilities of Inuit women were the same wherever or with whomever they were living. However, in spite of the hard work necessary to keep families warm and well fed, their homes were always filled with laughter. The Inuit adored their children, cuddling them when they were very young and playing games with them as they grew up. Boys began to hunt by their early teens and would marry before they were twenty years old, or as soon as they had proven their ability to feed a family. Girls were often married by the age of fourteen.

Story Sources

The Inuit had no written language until the 1960s, when a series of standard writing systems was developed for the people of Greenland, Canada, and Alaska. Many people still speak their native languages, all of which belong to a subfamily of the Eskimo-Aleut language family. From eastern Alaska, across the northern Arctic to Greenland, the Inuit speak Inupiak (called Inuktitut in Nunavut, Canada, and Kalaallisut in Greenland). In Alaska, people speak both Inupiak and Yupik, two languages that are as different as French and Italian.[6]

The earliest and largest collections of Inuit stories were made during the late nineteenth and early twentieth centuries by three men: Knud Rasmussen, Henry Rink, and Franz Boas. They wanted to put the stories down on paper before the old storytellers were all gone. Rasmussen and Rink recorded many myths while traveling in Greenland and Canada, and Boas recorded stories in eastern Canada. The published works of these men remain the primary sources for Inuit stories today. Rasmussen found that the best stories were told by old Inuit shamans, some of whom were amused by his notebook and pencil. One shaman said, "From what you say, it would seem that folk in that far country of yours 'eat' talk marks just as we eat caribou meat."[7]

It is easy to imagine Inuit families snuggled together in their winter houses listening to storytellers fill the long winter months with dramatic tales of magic and adventure. Storytellers told two kinds of stories: ancient ones and recent stories. Ancient stories were about a time when unbelievable things could happen. They told about encounters with animals in human form, and about witches and sea goddesses. Recent tales included the adventures of hunters on land and sea–stories about courage, strength, vanity, and conceit.

Storytellers broke up the monotony of long hours spent indoors in winter darkness by telling and retelling their favorite adventure stories. These were often long straightforward sagas that continued on for many nights and could be picked up and dropped at any point in the telling. Each storyteller made his particular version of a story as exciting and entertaining as he was able. One explorer observed, ". . . some [stories] are almost wholly related in verse or musical form; others are told in prose, with every sort of appropriate gesture, modulation of the voice, and facial expression. A number of them are onomatopoeic in character, imitating the calls and cries of birds and creatures of the wild."[8]

Inuit children understood they were loved and adored, and they were secure in that love. Stories, though often frightening, always had a cultural focus. For example, a story in which a father schemed to kill his son was not really about the father's treachery, but about the power of an amulet. Likewise, a story in which a father cut off his daughter's fingers to save himself from an angry sea was less about that gruesome act, and more about all the sea animals that were created from the joints of the young girl's fingers. The girl became a goddess who was worshiped for having provided a bountiful supply of sea animals.

The Inuit peacefully settled arguments by arranging singing duels whereby two enemies faced each other before an audience. Each person took a turn singing songs about the other's misdeeds. The duel ended when one of the opponents ran out of accusations. He became the loser. Therefore, in the kind of society that arranges singing duels to avoid violence, it would seem that tales of violence belonged to the realm of the imagination.

Contact and Change

Beginning in the 1500s, European explorers came to Greenland and Canada seeking a northwest passage to the Orient. These explorers tried futilely for hundreds of years to sail through the frozen waters of the north before they realized that this was not the route to the Orient. Many of them stayed and established whaling stations and trading posts. As one scholar noted, "In the course of the most magnificent failure in navigational history, Westerners met Eskimos time and again."[9]

By the early 1700s, Denmark had laid claim to Greenland in the eastern Arctic, and fifty years later Russia laid claim to Alaska in the western Arctic.

Long after Native Americans and the Inuit migrated across the Bering Strait, another and different group of people, the Aleut, migrated across the strait. I include the Aleut in this book so that their history and stories will not be forgotten. Ancestors of the Aleut settled on Unangan Island, one of the many islands in the Aleutian chain of islands that extends from the Alaska Peninsula into the Pacific Ocean. They spoke their own language, Aleut, had a strict class system that recognized chieftains, and they owned slaves. In the mid 1700s, the Aleuts welcomed the arrival of Russian explorers, but soon the strangers dominated the islands and forced Aleut men to hunt sea mammals for the Russian fur trade. Before long, extremely cruel treatment at the hands of the Russians and epidemics of smallpox and influenza greatly reduced the Aleut population.[10]

In 1867, the United States purchased from Russia the present-day territory of Alaska, which included the Aleutian Islands. Thirteen years later, in 1880, Great Britain transferred ownership of the eastern Arctic Islands to Canada.

A significant sign of unity among people of the Arctic was expressed in 1977 at a Circumpolar Conference held in Great Barrows, Alaska. At that time, all the people of the

Arctic, from Alaska in the west to Greenland in the east, agreed to replace the word Eskimo with the term Inuit.[11]

Then, in 1996, the Canadian government established the territory of Nunavut, which means "our land," in Inuktitut. Nunavut was carved out of the central and eastern areas of Canada's Northwest Territories where 80 percent of the population is Inuit. The Inuit are now represented in Canada's national government affairs, and in the future they will manage wildlife resources, and have the right to hunt and fish throughout the region.[12]

Although there are seven major dialect groupings of Inuktitut in the territory of Nunavut, the Inuit who live in Canada understand each other and can communicate with their Greenlander neighbors. After a few days or a week their ears can also pick up the Yupik language spoken by their Alaskan neighbors. (In Greenland, children born of parents who were of mixed European and Inuit blood were referred to as "Greenlanders.")[13]

Stories in this Book

The stories in this book are told as closely as possible to the original translations. It is difficult to judge their full meaning because they were created within the framework of another, very different culture. Yet they resemble myths the world over in which magic plays a major role and adventurers are great heroes. The geographic sources for these stories are roughly divided among the Inuit of Greenland, Canada, and Alaska. These three Arctic regions are governed by different nations: Greenland by Denmark; Nunavut by Canada; and Alaska by the United States. Because each of these regions includes a wide variety of environments, I have taken two stories from each country, plus one from the Aleutian Islands.

Preceding each story is an introduction explaining the particular environment and lifestyles of the people at the time the story was being recorded. Throughout this book I have used the term Inuit. However, quotations cannot be altered, and the reader must bear in mind that the sections of Expert Commentary that are included at the end of each story were written long before the term Inuit had replaced the word Eskimo.

"The Woman Who Adopted a Bear" is an ancient story from Polar Greenland. It is a tale of love, anger, and revenge in which a small polar bear cub develops human qualities.[14]

The west Greenland story, "The Girl Who Married a Gnome," is about a dwarf who marries a local girl. Gnomes are mythological characters who appear as humans in Inuit stories. They have all the characteristics of people, but they are only about a foot in height. Gnomes were seldom seen, except by shamans, and were known to be strong and quick. They lived on land and sea, and if one chose to capture a man, he might never be released.[15]

"The Adventures of Kivioq" is a long saga about a young hero who encounters witches, murderers, and animals in human form. He is rescued by his spirit helper, Snow Bunting, a small white bird that spends the summer in the Arctic. There are many versions throughout the Arctic of Kivioq's adventures, but I have chosen only a small part of the saga recorded by Rasmussen during his travels in Canada.[16]

Sedna was a mythological goddess who ruled over the sea world. Long ago, she was a beautiful young woman, but her father chopped off her fingers to save himself from an angry sea god. Often an *angatok*, or shaman, visited her at the bottom of the sea and combed her long hair because she had no fingers.[17]

The adventures of Oogoon in Alaska are similar to Kivioq's adventures in Baffinland, except Oogoon lives in an inland environment where some Inuit never visit the sea, hunt sea mammals, or live in snow houses. In "Oogoon's Adventures on the Kobuk River," he is rescued by his spirit-helper, an ermine, or type of weasel. Oogoon's spirit-helper saves him from encounters with a cannibalistic witch, a bear in human form, and an evil old man.[18]

Many stories have been recorded by Inuit groups along the coast of Alaska. One of the more popular stories is about Kinak, the Hill Giant. The Hill Giant lays sprawled across Alaska's frozen tundra forming low hills and breathing bad weather. He befriends a battered woman and later kills her unworthy son. It is a tale about the banishment of this young man.[19]

The Aleut story "Ol-an-uk the Orphan" is about how a young boy lived all alone on a wind-blown Aleutian island after his parents disappeared. It is a story of loss, loneliness, competition, and love.[20]

Today

Now the Inuit live in much the same way as the Danes, Canadians, Americans, and other foreigners who have come to live among them, and few vestiges of traditional life remain.

Sealing, whaling, and walrus-hunting remain important activities in Greenland (although today, hunting is for meat and not for skins). The fishing industry is Greenland's most important means of support, and in the subarctic regions of the southernmost part of the island, Greenlanders have also established large sheep farms.[21]

In Alaska, fishing remains an important part of the

state's economy. Tourism and the petroleum and mining industries currently provide many jobs for native people.[22]

While some men still hunt and fish in the old way, other men, and women, are preserving the old traditions by illustrating them in blocks of native soapstone. Soapstone is no longer being used to make bowls and pots. Instead, it is being carved by gifted artists into valuable art objects that are collected by people all over the world. The carvings depict men brandishing harpoons, hunters in kayaks, and women carrying young children in the hoods of their anoraks, and they also represent the native seals, whales, and walruses. Such lifelike images of the Inuit people and the animals of the Arctic are reminders of the rich cultural heritage.

Today, Inuit children study their native languages and customs in schools, and storytelling remains an important teaching tool. By keeping the old stories alive, we also keep open the great windows to the Arctic past.

1

THE WOMAN WHO ADOPTED A BEAR

POLAR INUIT OF NORTHERN GREENLAND

INTRODUCTION

The Inuit who lived closest to the North Pole were called the Polar Inuit. They lived farther north than any other humans in the world—on the very tip of Greenland—an island almost completely buried beneath a permanent layer of ice and snow. Winter in northern Greenland is long, cold, and dark. Summer is short and cool. The sea remains frozen nine months of the year, and for four of those months, it is also too dark to hunt. Northern Greenland experiences the harshest weather conditions in all of the Arctic, yet for the Polar Inuit, the land and sea held few secrets.

When European explorers first encountered the Polar Inuit in the early 1800s, there were between two hundred and two hundred fifty people living in the Arctic's harshest environment on the northern tip of Greenland. These people believed they were the only humans in the world and looked upon the white explorers as gods from the sky. In Baffinland, when the Inuit first met John Ross and his men, they asked, "Who are you? What are you? Where do you come from? Is it from the sun or the moon?"[1]

The Polar Inuit survived by hunting seals in winter, white whales and narwhals in summer, polar bears in fall, and walruses year round. During the warm months, they hunted caribou, fox, and hares on land and fished along the rocky shores. The Polar Inuit did not fish or hunt from boats because neither the sea ice nor the ice in the fjords—the deep, rocky, water-filled canyons along the coast—completely melted during the short summer months. However, after the kayak was introduced into the region by some Canadian Inuit in 1860, the Polar Inuit learned to hunt by boat and to dodge floating ice.

The Polar Inuit lived most of the year in igloos, or snow houses, out on the frozen sea ice. It took a skilled house-builder a couple of hours to build an igloo large enough to accommodate his family.

A long tunnel led from inside the igloo to the outdoors. It was cut into the snow below the level of the igloo's doorway. Since the tunnel was lower than the floor of the igloo, and because hot air rises, the tunnel kept the warm air inside the igloo from escaping. When more than one large family traveled together, they often built similar style tunnels at ground level to connect their houses so they could visit back and forth without going out-of-doors.

Inside the igloo, women kept blubber burning in sturdy soapstone lamps that provided light and warmth, and fire for cooking. Above the lamp, a thin soapstone roasting pot filled with meat was hung from a wooden rack. The meat was cooked slowly over the fire for several hours.

Families often had to move during the winter in search of seals. Then women would pack the families' belongings onto their dogsleds and follow the men in search of a new hunting territory. A recently abandoned igloo could belong to the next person or family who claimed it. Igloos eventually melted during the summer, and families had to build new ones each winter.

Families who did not hunt seals out on the frozen sea in winter lived in stone houses built on land. Stones of all sizes were plentiful along the Arctic coasts, and a group of men could easily build a long rectangular house in one day. This type of house could accommodate several extended families. The stone houses remained empty in summer and, in winter, could be claimed by the first family, or group of families, who moved into an empty one.

From May to September, during the warm months,

everyone lived along the coast in small tent-like structures covered with one or two layers of sealskin.

Personal possessions consisted of clothing and cooking implements; dwellings, hunting grounds, and food belonged to the group.[2]

The Polar Inuit listened to more stories than any other Arctic people because they experienced the longest period of darkness. To make the days go more quickly, storytellers kept people entertained with stories about spring and summer, warmth and sunshine. These stories always made people happy because they reminded people of the many friends they would see again in the summer, when the rocky coast was free of snow and the sea ice was breaking up. Favorite stories always revolved around a struggle to obtain food, whether the struggle was a competition between two men, or between man and beast.

The struggle to obtain a wife was nowhere so severe as it was in Polar Greenland where the population was very small. In the beginning of the story called "The Woman Who Adopted a Bear," one man kills another to take his wife. Opening a story with a murder was a convenient beginning for storytellers; it allowed them to create a variety of serial episodes whereby others in the story would seek vengeance for the killing. In this story, villagers are the ones seeking vengeance, not for the murder, but because the killer had robbed them of a great hunter.

The point of the story, however, was that in Inuit society laziness would not be tolerated. Laziness could mean the difference between life and death, and any member of a group who would not contribute had to be banished or killed. In this story, all of the men in the village became lazy; thus they all had to be punished by death.

In this story, the Inuit respect for animals was

demonstrated after an old lady adopted a young bear cub and treated him like a grandson. Likewise, spirit-power was at work when the spirit of a young boy entered the body of a dead animal, allowing the animal to keep the boy's grandmother well fed.

The form of the story allowed for subsequent episodes: since the hero killed a man to take his wife, a new, related episode could have provided the opportunity for the murdered man's family to seek revenge. However, instead, the story ended decisively after the hero and his stolen bride settled down in the village where the hero had been born. The hero's family became the ancestors of a family known throughout the region for their hunting abilities.[3]

THE WOMAN WHO ADOPTED A BEAR

Long ago, there lived a successful hunter with a reputation for generosity. Hungry strangers came from far and wide to request meat and skins from Angudluk, the great hunter. Angudluk packed the strangers' sleds with seal meat and skins and sent them away, saying, "I am sorry I have so little to give. These provisions are from spoiled animals, and my wife has done a poor job of preparing them. They are yours if you will accept them."

Angudluk's wife watched as her husband's chest puffed out with pride when the strangers thanked him for his generosity. She remembered the long nights she spent removing blubber from the sealskins to make them soft and pliable. Angudluk's wife envied the wives of unsuccessful hunters who did not have to work so hard, and she sulked about her own predicament. The more she sulked, however, the more choice pieces of seal meat she popped into her mouth. Soon she became very fat, and people stopped to stare at her as she passed.

"Why should we work so hard for those women whose husbands cannot bring home seals?" she asked her mother-in-law.

"My son is a great hunter," replied the mother-in-law.

"And he is a generous man who gets pleasure from sharing his surpluses." Angudluk's wife frowned and walked away.

One day a stranger named Tuku came to their village. Tuku had recently lost his wife in a sledding accident and wanted to find another. "I will inquire for you on my journeys," Angudluk told Tuku. A man was not allowed to hunt for one month after he had touched a corpse; therefore, the stranger was prevented from joining Angudluk on his upcoming hunting expedition.

One day, while the women of the village played a game of toss-ball, Tuku stopped in to see Angudluk's wife. She was still working, cleaning animals from her husband's latest hunt. "I am sorry that you are not playing games with

the other women," Tuku said. "I would so enjoy seeing your pretty movements jumping and chasing the ball."

Angudluk's wife grew sad and told the stranger, "I have not played ball since I was a girl. Instead, day after day I must stay indoors scraping blubber off all these sealskins. My fingers were once long and thin. Now they are stubby and scarred from so much scraping. I do not play any more."

Tuku pretended to be sympathetic. He had learned what he had set out to know—that Angudluk's wife was dissatisfied with her life. They chatted and laughed together until evening. Then Tuku set out to meet Angudluk and help him bring home his catch.

Tuku walked until he heard the sounds of the proud

hunter's sled gliding across the snow with its load of seals. He waited until Angudluk came within close range, then raised his harpoon and thrust it straight into the hunter's chest.

"You make your wife work too hard," he shouted as Angudluk fell onto the frozen ice. "You will never do that again."

When Tuku returned to the village driving Angudluk's sled, the people understood at once what had happened. But they were afraid of the stranger and said nothing.

At last, the villagers went to Angudluk's house and found only his mother and his young son, Ituko. The stranger, Tuku, had run away with Angudluk's fat wife.

The villagers, fearing they might go hungry without Angudluk to feed them, now boldly raided the meat racks behind his house. Since they could not take all the meat at once, they returned day after day for more.

One day, the old grandmother greeted one of the women who came to take meat. "Oh, if only there will be enough meat left to feed young Ituko until spring when I can go up into the cliffs and catch young auk birds," she sighed.

The woman went home and repeated the grandmother's words to her husband. "She is right," he said. "Soon there will be no meat for any of us. We must find that stranger who killed Angudluk and ended our plentiful supply of meat. We must seek revenge."

So the woman's angry husband organized the men of the village, and together they set out to find the stranger. Barely had they left home when they found Angudluk's frozen body lying on the ice. Nearby, they discovered two seals that the murderer had thrown from the sled to lighten his load. Even though it was customary to bury a person on land under a pile of stones, the men agreed not to bring

Angudluk's body back to the village where seeing it would renew everyone's sorrow and anger. So they stuffed the frozen body down within a large crack in the ice, loaded the two discarded seals onto the sled, and returned to the village. The men were ashamed at the untraditional way they had disposed of Angudluk's body, but they were pleased that they had two fat seals to take home.

As the men came into the village, the women ran out to greet them. "I see there was good luck hunting seals today," cried one of the women. The men smiled proudly.

The women had not noticed that the seals their husbands carried on the sled were frozen. Seals must come up to breathe at regular intervals during the day. To do so, they make holes in the ice and keep the holes open by breaking each new layer of ice that forms on top. It would have taken several days for a freshly killed seal to freeze once it had been harpooned and taken out of the water. If the women had looked, they would have seen that the seals the hunters brought home had not been freshly harpooned.

Suddenly, however, a small voice came from the crowd. "It is not often that the seals come frozen to their blow holes." It was Ituko, Angudluk's young son, who had spoken. Ituko had the wisdom of a great hunter even though he was still a young boy.

The "hunter" whose chest was most puffed up by the delivery of two large seals now became enraged. He took out his snow knife, rushed over to the boy, and struck him in the head. Ituko fell dead on the ground.

"You have taken all I have in life," cried Angudluk's mother. "First my son disappears, and now my only grandson is killed." The old woman picked up the little boy's limp body, carried it home, and sang the boy's favorite songs for five long days.

Finally, the old woman laid her grandson on the little sled that he had used to bring home chunks of freshwater ice from the fjords to be melted for cooking and drinking. She pulled the little boy's body far up a nearby fjord where she buried his small body under a pile of rocks.

The old lady returned home at the same time hunters arrived with a sled carrying a live polar bear cub and the carcass of a large adult bear. When the old lady saw the little cub, she pleaded with the hunters to let her adopt him. "Please give me the bear cub. He will be my adopted grandson."

The hunters mumbled among themselves. "Let's give her the cub until he is big and fat. Then we will take him back," whispered one of the men, and the others agreed. The old lady went home, hugging the little cub against her body. Thereafter, the furry white cub and the old lady were inseparable. They ate, played, and slept together. In the evening, Angudluk's mother sang to the cub the songs her son and grandson had loved to hear.

Before long, Angudluk's great store of meat began to run out, and the old lady worried that she and her cub would soon have nothing left to eat. Then, one day the old lady heard the hunters complaining. "That cub eats too much," said one of the men. "It is time we added him to our store of meat before he eats up all the rest."

After supper that night, the old lady wrapped meat in a large sealskin pouch and said to the cub. "We must leave the village right away. We will go far up into the fjord on the opposite side of the bay where the men cannot find us."

The old woman and the young bear cub traveled all night under a bright star-lit sky. Finally, they settled into a shallow cave high up in the steep rock walls of the fjord. Each day the young cub went hunting and brought home a seal. Soon the old woman had so much meat that she took

only her favorite parts from the animals: fresh warm livers, brains, and hearts. And the pile of decaying carcasses grew higher and higher.

But one day, when men from the village were passing some distance below the cave, their dogs smelled the decaying meat and led them up the side of the fjord. "Well," said one of the men, spying the pile of dead animals, "someone eats very well."

The old lady stood up straight and tall and planted her thin arms firmly on her hips. "Go away," she commanded defiantly. "This is our home now. We want to be left alone."

A thin scraggly man, his head hung downward, spoke in a quiet voice. "We are all very hungry. Angudluk took such good care of us and fed us so well that we do not remember how to hunt. Perhaps if you return to the village the young cub will teach us."

The old woman could see that the men were starving, and she felt sorry for them. She also missed her old home. So she agreed to return.

Shortly after the old lady and her cub settled into their old home, a man from the village came. He told the bear it was time for him to go hunting. Dutifully, the young cub headed off onto the sea ice, but none of the men ever joined him. That evening he brought home two fat seals. Every day thereafter men from the village came and told the cub to go hunting. Each day the little cub went hunting alone.

Soon the villagers grew fat and lazy. Men played games and gossiped with the women while the young cub did the work of feeding the villagers.

Despite all the cub's work, however, the old lady was given only a small portion of each day's catch, and she missed her favorite foods. One day she asked the young cub to bring her the fin of a narwhal, which she had not tasted for a long time. The cub returned early that day dragging a huge narwhal behind him. He lumbered on past the villagers and went straight home. He dropped the narwhal in front of his grandmother's little stone house and stood guard over it until she came out to claim her favorite fin.

"He has become too impertinent," said one of the men. "And he is so big that he can hurt us if he gets angry. I think it is time to kill him."

Forgetting that without the bear they would all starve to death, the men agreed to kill him. The idea excited them so much, in fact, that they rushed at the young cub and hurled spears into his back, head, and chest. The poor young animal toppled over onto the ground and stopped breathing.

When the old lady saw what had happened she rushed out the door and threw herself on top of her precious cub. "Oh," she sobbed. "Now I have lost my dear adopted son. I am too old to live alone. Kill me," she begged the hunters. "Kill me, too."

For a brief moment the hunters felt shame. But the feeling quickly passed, and they ran home to get their knives to cut up the carcass of the young bear. The first hunter drove his knife into the bear's chest to get his heart, but quickly jumped backward in horror when he saw Ituko emerge from inside the bear's skin.

"I took the shape of a bear to feed my grandmother," said Ituko to the hunter. "And I have fed all of you as well. But you were so greedy you killed me all over again. Have you no shame?"

Then Ituko grabbed a spear and thrust it clear through the chest of the man who stood before him. When the others started to run away, he speared them, too, three and four at a time.

"We were only playing a joke," said one of the remaining men. "Please do not kill all of us. We will throw a big party and welcome you home."

The man's whining only made Ituko angrier, and he raged through the village killing all the inhabitants, even the dogs who had nipped at his paws when he was a young cub. Ituko was so furiously filled with anger and revenge that when his grandmother came out of the house to greet him, he accidentally killed her, too.

As soon as he realized what he had done, Ituko fell onto his knees and wept.

The following day Ituko took his grief up into the cave in the fjord where as a young cub he had lived with his grandmother. He mourned for many days to dispel his emotions. Then, he began to hunt.

When peace finally came to Ituko, his cave was filled with meat. But he realized he needed a wife to scrape and sew his animal skins. So one day he set out and walked until he came upon a small settlement. The people were kind but old, and he did not see a wife among them. As he prepared to leave, an old man spoke, "My son is coming home with his new wife tonight," he said. "They are young like you. You should stay and meet them."

Ituko agreed to go out and meet the bride and groom. Not far from the settlement he saw the couple's sled approaching. "Get out of my way, " cried the proud young man whose sled was pulled by many dogs. "Can't you see I have brought home a new wife?"

Ituko ignored the brash groom's warning and stared at the beautiful young girl on the sled. He suddenly wanted her more than he had ever wanted anyone in his life. Without warning, Ituko pulled out his knife and, with one powerful jab, drove it into the chest of the arrogant young groom and killed him. Ituko jumped onto the sled, turned it around, and headed back to his old village, pulling the young bride, now a widow, along with him.

After they pulled up in front of the house Ituko had shared with his parents and grandmother, the young bride spoke for the first time, "Where have you taken me?" she asked. "This place is deserted. It is a terrible village."

Ituko showed the girl the cache of meat and animal skins he had accumulated while mourning, and she realized at once that she was in the presence of a great hunter.

The beautiful young girl and Angudluk's son raised a family and lived in the village for many happy years.

QUESTIONS AND ANSWERS

Q: *What kind of houses did the Polar Inuit occupy in the winter?*

A: They lived in snow houses, or igloos, out on the frozen sea ice, and stone houses on the land.

Q: *What type of dwelling did they use in summer?*

A: They lived in skin-covered tent-style shelters on land.

Q: *Why did Angudluk give away his meat surpluses?*

A: He was a very successful hunter and wanted to show off his skills. He also had a generous nature.

Q: *How did the stranger, Tuku, kill Angudluk, and why?*

A: Tuku went out to meet Angudluk when he returned from hunting and stabbed him. He wanted to steal Angudluk's wife.

Q: *What was the burial custom of the people, and why did Angudluk fail to receive a proper burial?*

A: It was customary for people to be buried under a large pile of stones on the mainland. The hunters in this story believed the people of the village would be upset by seeing Angudluk's body, so they shoved it through a crack in the ice.

Q: *Why did the men of the village kill Angudluk's son, Ituko?*

A: The boy was smart enough to notice that the hunters had lied about having killed the seals they brought back to the village. Therefore, the hunters feared that Ituko would probably also figure out that they had lied about the fate of his father.

Q: What did Ituko's grandmother do with her grandson's body?

A: After singing his favorites songs for five days, she took his body up into the fjord and gave him a proper burial under a pile of stones.

Q: Why did Ituko's grandmother adopt the polar bear cub?

A: After her son and grandson were killed, she was left alone. The cub gave her a reason to live.

Q: Why did Ituko kill everyone in his village?

A: He was filled with so much anger for what had been done to his father and to himself, not only as a young boy but also in the form of a bear, that he went crazy.

Q: How did Ituko finally find a wife?

A: He went out to greet a young groom and his bride returning home to their village and immediately fell in love with the beautiful young bride. He killed the groom and took the girl home to his old village.

EXPERT COMMENTARY

Knud Rasmussen was born in Greenland. His parents were of mixed European and Inuit blood, and he was considered a "Greenlander." Rasmussen became fluent in the Inupiak language before his family moved to Denmark when he was seven years old. Rasmussen returned to Greenland as part of a scientific expedition in 1902. He traveled all across the Arctic, recording the myths and legends of the people, and eventually he married an Inuit woman. Rasmussen's heritage and command of the language enabled him to meet and talk with storytellers unavailable to outsiders. His published stories remain the primary source of Inuit myths today. He says about the people's struggle for survival:

> The harsh conditions of nature which force the Eskimos into an unending fight for existence, quickly teach him to take hold of life with a practical grip—i.e., in order to live I must first of all have food! And as he finds himself in the happy position that this form of livelihood—hunting—is also his supreme passion, one is justified in saying that he leads a happy life, content with the portion that fate has allotted to him. He is born with the qualities necessary for the winning of his livelihood, and the skill in handling the tools, which later on makes a master of him, he acquires through play while he grows up. On the day when he can measure his strength with that of the men, he takes a wife and enters the ranks of the hunters. [4]

Rasmussen asked a Polar Inuit man about his religious beliefs, and the Inuit replied:

> 'We do not believe in any God, as you do,' said he. 'We do not all understand the hidden things, but we believe the people who say they do. We believe our Angakuit [angotak], our magicians, and we believe them because

we wish to live long, and because we do not want to expose ourselves to the danger of famine and starvation. We believe, in order to make our lives and our food secure. If we did not believe the magicians, the animals we hunt would make themselves invisible to us; if we did not follow their advice, we should fall ill and die.'[5]

Many Inuit groups practiced infanticide, the killing of babies after birth. They killed the female babies to insure the survival of families and communities because male babies were more important to the group as future hunters. Rasmussen says:

> The most glaring consequence of the struggle for existence is manifested in the way in which they try to breed the greatest possible number of boys and the fewest possible girls. For it is solely economy that lies behind the custom that girls are killed at birth, if they have not already been promised to a family where there is a son who some day is to have a wife. These murders of newborn girls are not at all committed as the outcome of crudeness of mind nor because they underrate the importance of the female in the community; they are quite well aware that she is indispensable. When it happens, it is only because the struggle for existence is so hard, because the experience of generations is that the individual provider is unable to feed more than the most necessary members of the family.
>
> The reasoning that lies behind infanticide is as follows: a female infant is only a trouble and an expense to the household as long as she cannot make herself useful. But the moment she is able to help she is married and leaves her own family; for it is the rule, that the woman goes with the family into which she has married. For this reason they try to regulate births in order to get as many boys as possible.[6]

2

THE GIRL WHO MARRIED A GNOME

INUIT OF WEST AND EAST GREENLAND

INTRODUCTION

Along Greenland's west coast, the island's giant ice cap rolls all the way down to the sea and separates the Polar Inuit from their neighbors to the south. Further south along the coast summers are a little longer and winter has fewer months of darkness. The snow begins to fall in September, and by October the sea is frozen solid. The earth does not come alive again until July or August.

Meltwater released from Greenland's giant ice cap carves hundreds of fjords into the land along the coast. The fjords, which break up the coastline, provide a constant source of fresh water for the people and a natural nesting place for migrating birds.

Like their neighbors to the north, many Inuit who inhabited this portion of Greenland's west coast lived in igloos, or winter houses made from blocks of snow, out on the frozen sea ice. If they remained on the land in winter, they lived in stone houses built along the shore.

Families looked forward to moving to a summer campsite in spring. When they sought a new site, they paddled up to a settlement and sat silently offshore. If the residents did not come out to greet them, the family paddled on. But if the residents beckoned them to come ashore, the family understood they were welcome at the site. At these summer sites, families set up simple shelters to use for sleeping and protection against inclement weather. Women kept busy sewing clothes out of the many sealskins obtained during the winter.

Men went fishing and hunting in kayaks along the coast or up into the fjords. Often whole families joined the men on their trips into the fjords. Then, the family traveled in a large umiak that held them and their supplies. Kayaks and umiaks were ideally suited for traveling in ice-filled waters because they were light enough to be pulled quickly out of the water to avoid floating ice.

Many Inuit families settled along the southwestern portion of the island where the sea does not freeze over in winter, yet is filled with floating ice in spring and summer. Ice that forms along the east coast of Greenland is carried down the east side of the island by the East Greenland current, around Cape Farewell on the tip of the island, and up along the western shores. Families often moved onto smaller islands off the west coast to hunt seals that rode the drifting ice masses.

In summer, hunters followed migrating herds of reindeer across the tundra as they fed on dense clumps of flowers, mosses, grasses, lichen, and fungi that pushed up through the melting snow.[1]

There were very few settlements along the eastern coast of Greenland because the island's ice cap covers most of the coastline and the huge masses of drifting ice, which flow down from the north, come close to the land. Still, some people settled in sheltered coves along the southeastern shore.[2]

In the story "The Girl Who Married a Gnome," the ever-present threat of starvation plays a prominent role, as it does in so many other Inuit stories. In this story, a disrespectful young man learned that intimidation and verbal threats would not always get him a wife. A mythological gnome appeared, married a young girl, and kept her family well fed. The appearance of a magical figure proved that sometimes a woman can survive quite well without being taken by force. The story also reminded its listeners of how important cooperation and sharing can be in an environment where the likelihood of starvation was always present.[3]

The Girl Who Married a Gnome

Arouk lived with her aged parents in a small sealskin summer tent close to the mouth of a great fjord. Many hunters who traveled up and down the fjord in summer stopped to visit Arouk, but her father always sent them away because he believed no man was good enough for his beautiful daughter. Arouk loved her parents, but she very much wanted to get married.

One day a young man paddled up to the shore and called, "Arouk. Arouk. Come out."

"Listen, father. He knows my name," said Arouk pushing aside the caribou-hide door cover of the tent to peek outside.

"Go away," yelled her father to the young man. "There is no one here by that name."

But the young man persisted. "I have seen Arouk. I know she is there," he yelled back. And then the brazen young man got out of his kayak and walked up to the little tent. The stranger's boldness made the old man angry.

"Go away," he said, and he pushed the young suitor backwards. But the young man caught himself, straightened up, and shoved the old man down onto the ground. Furious that a young man would show such a lack of respect, Arouk's father picked up a rock and threw it. The rock struck the young suitor on the head, and he fell to the ground unconscious.

"Oh, my," the father muttered. "What have I done?" The old man suddenly feared for his life. He called to his wife and daughter and told them to pack up the family's belongings and hurry down to the shore. The family loaded up their little umiak, and left as quickly as possible.

On shore, the young suitor, who had regained consciousness, jumped up and shouted, "You will be sorry, old man. Your daughter will never find a husband, and you will starve before I or any other man gives you food."

The old man, his wife, and their beautiful daughter traveled for many hours before they spotted a small island far away from the mainland and went ashore. Half hidden behind a giant boulder sat an abandoned stone house that suited them quite well.

The family lived happily in the little house until one day, when the old man began to have visions. "This morning I saw a little man in our house," he said to his wife and daughter. Arouk shrugged her shoulders and continued to cut up seal meat for the evening meal.

Again the next morning, Arouk's father saw the little man reaching up toward Arouk's sealskin lamp to warm his tiny hands. But when the father got down from the sleeping platform, the little man was gone. "I am certain there was a little man standing here just a minute ago," he said to Arouk.

At last the daughter spoke: "Father, I have married an *atliarusek* [an Inuit word for elf or gnome]. But I feared you would not like him, so I do not let him stay long in our house."

The old man thought this news over. Finally, he said, "I do not mind. Tell him to come and live with us."

The following morning when Arouk's father woke up he saw the stout little man sitting on the platform beside his daughter. He was pleased to have a new son-in-law, even if he was very small.

That evening Arouk' s husband brought home a stack of fresh seals. "My husband has brought us meat," she told her father, "but he must take some home to his relatives, and we will not see him for awhile."

A long time passed before the *atliarusek* returned, but finally one morning when the old man awoke, his elusive son-in-law was resting comfortably beside his daughter. The old man smiled and laid back down on his furry caribou blanket. For many months the stout little man sat beside Arouk in the morning, but he always disappeared before the family got up. One morning, however, the *atliarusek* did not disappear. He stayed home all day. "I am resting," he told his father-in-law. "Tomorrow I must go to the mainland and visit my people."

"We will join you," said the old man.

"No, it is a very long trip," said the *atliarusek* staring up into his father-in-law's anxious face. "I must travel far up a long fjord, and it takes many days."

Arouk stopped mending her father's caribou-skin anorak. "We would all like to join you," she said to her husband. "We are hardy people."

Eventually, the *atliarusek* agreed to let his wife and her parents follow him in their umiak. They set off the next day, but the family had to paddle very hard to keep up with the *atliarusek's* little kayak as it skimmed expertly over the water. That evening when they stopped to rest, a series of tiny kayaks carrying other *atliaruseks* joined them. And each day thereafter, whenever they stopped to rest, more kayaks filled with the little people got in line behind them.

One afternoon, Arouk's husband pulled up beside the

old man's boat and said, "We are going to disappear so
that people on land do not see us. Stay in the wake of our
boats." Then, all of the boats disappeared under the sea.

"This is very frightening," said the old man to his
daughter. "Perhaps we should not have followed your
atliarusek husband." But before he could say another
word, their umiak dove underwater and resurfaced at a
place beyond where they could be seen from the shore.

Arouk's family followed the long line of *atliarusek*
kayaks up a narrow fjord. When at last they stopped, they
had to tie up their boats onto large boulders sticking up out
of the water. The *atliaruseks* stopped below a steep cliff
where a progression of natural steps made it easier for

them to climb to the top. Even so, the *atliarusek* had to reach above their heads, grab the edge of each step above them, and pull themselves up, one step at a time. Arouk and her family followed after them.

Arouk and her parents followed the *atliaruseks* far inland until they came to the Valley of the Caribou where thousands of large brown caribou fed on stubby willow trees and clumps of grey-green grass that grew where the snow had melted. "You may stay here and I will hunt with you," said the *atliarusek* to his wife and her parents.

The family hunted caribou all summer with the *atliarusek* people and filled their umiak with meat and furs to take home. When it was time to leave, they bade

goodbye to their new friends and headed down the fjord and back out to the sea. Now, even if the seals stayed away the following winter, the family would not go hungry.

Not long after they arrived home, a hunter from their old village came to visit. The visitor told Arouk's family that his people at home were starving. The old man grew silent after he heard the news. His family had enjoyed great prosperity during the summer, and he knew he should share it with his old friends. So he loaded up his boat with caribou meat and hides and journeyed back to his old village. When he pulled up to shore, his boat overflowing with fresh meat, the men scorned him. "You expect us to believe you got this yourself?" asked the young man who had tried to steal Arouk from her family. "You would not allow your daughter to marry; therefore you cannot have anyone to secure meat for you. You could not have taken all this caribou meat by yourself!"

The old man remained silent as he unloaded the meat on shore for his old friends, got back into his boat, and paddled home. Before long, Arouk's husband returned home and heard the story about the ungrateful friends. "Invite them to our island. We will show them our prosperity."

The old man did as his son-in-law requested—he returned to his old village and invited the men to his island for a feast. Soon a long line of kayaks, many carrying his daughter's old suitors, pulled up along the shore. Arouk's family invited them in and prepared a great feast of caribou meat and seal blubber. After everyone had eaten, the old man stood up and spoke.

"Do you remember a long time ago one of you wanted my daughter for your wife? And do you remember that I had to flee from our village with my family because that suitor would not respect an old man and might have killed him? And that same young man prophesied that my daughter would never find a clever husband? Well, here sitting among you is my son-in-law who is a very great hunter," and the old man pointed to the *atliarusek*.

The men lowered their heads in shame.

"And does one of you remember that he vowed never to feed us if we were starving?"

Still, the men sat in silence. Not one of them raised his head—especially not the young man who was guilty of having made the threat.

The old man stood proudly before the group. "A father knows the man his daughter should marry," he said. "You see that I have made the right decision." Then, the old man's voice softened, and his words came forth gently. "Help yourself," he said. "Eat as much as you like."

QUESTIONS AND ANSWERS

Q: *The Polar Inuit lived on the northern tip of Greenland. Identify the main regions of Greenland south of that where there were other Inuit settlements.*

A: Some Inuit settled along the central portion of the west coast, but the largest settlements were along the southwestern coast. On the east side of Greenland, most Inuit lived up small inlets along the southeastern shores.

Q: *What causes great ice masses to fill the waters along the southwestern portion of Greenland?*

A: The East Greenland current brings ice down along the eastern side of the island, around Cape Farewell at the tip of the island, and up along the west coast.

Q: *Explain why Arouk and her family left their home on the mainland.*

A: Arouk's father had struck one of his daughter's suitors on the head with a rock and feared the young man might try to kill him.

Q: *What made Arouk's atliarusek husband different from other suitors?*

A: He was a gnome.

Q: *Why did Arouk and her family follow the atliarusek to the mainland?*

A: They wanted to hunt with him. And they may have been curious about where he lived.

Q: *How did the family learn that the people in their old village were starving?*

A: A passerby stopped at their island and reported the bad news.

Q: *Why did Arouk's father offer to feed the ungrateful villagers whom the family had left behind?*

A: Like all Inuit, Arouk's father understood the threat of starvation and felt sorry for them. But he also wanted to teach the young men of the village that they must respect their elders. And that no matter how angry a man might become, he should always remain generous.

Q: *What other lessons did the father wish to teach Arouk's old suitor and his villagers?*

A: The father can best choose his daughter's husband. And, finally, one should not curse another person with the threat of starvation; the curse might backfire and fall on the person who uttered it.

EXPERT COMMENTARY

Dr. Asen Balikci, a professor at the University of Montreal and a former staff member of the National Museum of Canada, has done extensive field work among the Inuit. He has completed nine films that record the seasonal camps of the Netsilik [who live in present-day Nunavut in Canada] during the 1950s and 1960s. About the *atliarusek*, he says:

> Inuarugligarsuit [*atliarusek*] are dwarfs living high up in the mountains. They have human figures and live exactly as Eskimos. The game they hunt is also tiny, their bears no bigger than lemmings. When seen by Eskimos, these dwarfs have the peculiar ability to grow in size up to the height of ordinary human beings.[4]

More than a half century ago, Norwegian historian Helge Ingstad lived among the Arctic Inuit and recorded many of their tales and traditions in her book *Nunamiut*. Ms. Ingstad describes their stories about dwarfs:

> Not infrequently, the Eskimos offer precise confirmation of what is told in a story. For example, they can tell of dwarfs so small that they sewed themselves anoraks from the skin of caribou ears, and they tell where the ruins of their habitations can be found. It looks as if many of the stories must contain a kernel of truth, but often imagination has spun a web round it that it is no longer visible.[5]

3

THE ADVENTURES OF KIVIOQ

NETSILIK OF NUNAVUT, CANADA

INTRODUCTION

The Netsilik lived in a vast area within the Canadian Arctic that extends from Committee Bay in the east to Victoria Strait in the west, and from Hudson Strait in the south to Bellot Strait in the north. Today the region is part of Nunavut, or "our land," a separate territory that was carved out of Canada's Northwest Territories in April 1999. It is a region of large land masses, with coastlines worn jagged by numerous ocean inlets, beyond which lie hundreds of small islands. Most of the region is very cold in winter, and cool and misty in summer.

The Netsilik say that long ago the Tunrit, a big and strong ancient people, first made their land habitable. The Tunrit built stone paths to lure caribou to water crossings where they could be easily trapped. The Tunrit also built stone weirs, arrangements of stones that resembled nets, along rivers and streams to catch migrating salmon. But the people were too timid and good-natured to defend their land from invasion, and they left after the Netsilik arrived.

In fall, when seals first begin to make breathing holes in the forming sea ice, the Netsilik set up large seal-hunting communities in the bays and inlets of the region. Some of the men guarded certain breathing holes, which forced the seals back into the water until they could resurface at breathing holes where hunters waited. Then the hunters would harpoon the emerging seals. During winter, families lived in igloos out on the sea ice or in stone houses on the land.

Families hunted caribou in July and August when herds of the huge animals headed south across the melting tundra, feeding on fresh moss and lichen. Women and children drove the herds into lakes; then men in kayaks speared them with long sharp lances. Durable caribou fur clothing kept the Netsilik warm in winter, and a successful hunt was important because it took six to eight hides to make one adult outfit. During summer, families lived in simple shelters covered with caribou skins.[1]

The Netsilik believed that the tundra was inhabited by dangerous and evil spirits, especially during the dark winter months when storytellers were concocting scary stories. There were many versions of the long saga about a young hero named Kivioq who helped his mother avenge the death of his father, and then narrowly escaped death at the hands of evil witches. The individual episodes that made up Kivioq's adventures, which appear to be unrelated, taught important lessons bound to the beliefs, traditions, and customs of the Netsilik. For example, listeners learned the value and origin of their magical amulets. Listeners also learned that witches had spirit-helpers that made them doubly dangerous, and they learned the origins of their terrain and traditions. The Netsilik credited an angry old witch who threw her knife across the water at Kivioq with having created the first icebergs, and they believed that their ancestors taught the wolves to hunt.

Kivioq's story ends after his wife is killed by her jealous mother. Kivioq paddles away and leaves his mother-in-law alone. Men in the Arctic might have gotten away with killing another man to get his wife, but prized and rare though they were, women were not strong enough to force a man to join them. Alone, Kivioq's mother-in-law would eventually die of starvation.[2]

THE ADVENTURES
OF KIVIOQ

Kivioq's father had been killed by an angry hunter several months before he was born. His mother vowed to avenge her husband's death and plotted to get even. Soon after the little boy was born, his mother wrapped his tiny body in the skin of a newborn seal and sewed it together so tightly that it fit just like his own. Kivioq's mother taught her young son how to hold his breath under water. They practiced each day until Kivioq grew so comfortable under water that his mother had to wait long periods of time for her young son to come up for air. One day Kivioq's mother said, "You are ready for the sea, my son." And she took him down to the shore. Kivioq's mother rubbed his sleek sealskin suit and smiled at her young son. "Swim out to sea," she said. "And when you see kayaks, show yourself above the water. The men will quickly paddle toward you. Let them come close, then duck under the water and hold your breath until you have led them far out to sea. After they are far enough away, I will raise a great storm, turn over their kayaks, and they will all drown."

Kivioq did as he was told and swam out to sea.

"Look," cried one hunter from his kayak. "There is a seal. Let's follow it."

Kivioq let the kayaks come close, then he dove down

under the water and disappeared. When he resurfaced, he was far out at sea, and the men's kayaks were right behind him. Kivioq quickly dove under the water again, and the men paddled rapidly after him.

Suddenly, an angry wind sent huge waves over the tops of the kayaks, and one by one, the little boats disappeared beneath the water. Only one kayak and hunter remained and continued to follow Kivioq. But soon this single hunter grew tired and stopped to rest. No sooner had he laid the paddle across his kayak than a great wave washed over him. Kivioq never saw the young hunter again.

Kivioq bobbed up and down in the water looking for more hunters until he was certain his mother had sought her complete revenge. Then he swam to the nearest island and went ashore. He found one small house, which had no windows or roof. Kivioq climbed up the wall of the house and looked down inside. An old witch sat on the sleeping platform tanning a human skin. From the top of the wall Kivioq blew down on the witch's head, then drew back so she could not see him. The witch looked up, but her thick wrinkled eyelids were so big and heavy that they fell down over her eyes and shrouded her sight. "Strange, my house has never leaked before," muttered the old witch.

Kivioq blew down on the witch again. This time she cut off her heavy eyelids with her tanning knife and looked up toward the top of the wall. Kivioq gasped at the sight of her hideous red-black eyes and let go his grip of the side of the house. He landed on the ground just in time for the old witch to greet him at the door. "Please come in," she said in a kind voice. "Let me hang up your clothes to dry."

Kivioq went inside and took off his wet clothing. The old witch hung the clothing on a long line that stretched across the room, and Kivioq jumped up onto the sleeping platform to stay warm.

"Wait here," said the old witch. "I must go out and get some more fuel for the fire."

Suddenly Kivioq began to fear that the old witch meant to cook him. He got down off the sleeping platform and began to poke around the room. "Oh," he gasped out loud as his hand brushed against a pile of human skulls. "What are these?" One of the skulls spoke up, "You had better get out of here in a hurry if you do not wish to join us!"

Kivioq reached for his clothing on the line above him. But each time he grabbed at his anorak, the line flew up into the air and out of reach. Desperate, Kivioq rubbed the small white feather that hung around his neck and called out to the bird who was his helping spirit, "Snow Bunting, Snow Bunting, where are you? Please help me."

Snow Bunting flew into the house and brushed her wings against the line that held Kivioq's clothing. The clothing fell to the floor, and Kivioq put it on as quickly as possible. Then he rushed out of the house, down to the shore, and jumped into the water.

Soon the old witch came running after him waving her long pointed knife. Frustrated that she could not reach him, but eager to show Kivok her great powers, the old witch gashed open a granite boulder on shore, just as easily as if she were cutting a piece of fresh meat.

Kivioq quickly responded by throwing his harpoon at an even larger boulder that jutted up out of the sea. The great stone split in two and fell into the water. "That is the way I would have harpooned you," cried Kivioq.

The old witch smiled gleefully. She was so impressed with Kivioq's great strength that she called out, "Please come back, I want you to be my husband."

Kivioq swam away as fast as he could go. The angry old witch hurled her knife after him. It skidded over the

water and eventually turned into a great ice floe. Thereafter, the sea began to freeze over every winter.

After Kivioq had escaped far from the angry witch, he stole a kayak and began to paddle from shore to shore in search of a place to settle. At first he stopped on a small island where two giant caterpillars, helping spirits of the old witch, tried to steal his kayak. He escaped just in time, back to the sea. Snow Bunting came to warn him that the witch had sent a giant clam after him, and Kivioq looked up just in time to dodge two huge shells that threatened to swallow him whole.

At last Kivioq returned home, but his mother was gone and the village was empty. He mourned for many months before he decided to seek a wife. Kivioq walked until he came upon a small stone house nestled against low-growing shrubs by the side of a lake. He called out, "Is anyone at home?" A sweet-looking old lady with graying hair came out to greet him. The old lady, who was really a wolf in human form, invited Kivioq in to meet her daughter. Kivioq entered the small stone house and was surprised to see that the daughter had the same graying hair as the mother, even though she was very young. After Kivioq had been with the women for two winters and had taught them how to hunt caribou, he asked the young girl to be his wife. Kiviok's young bride had become an excellent hunter, but her mother was too old to run fast and seldom brought down an animal.

In the evening Kivioq brought caribou home in his kayak, and his young wife waded out into the lake to retrieve the dead animals. Kivioq admired his wife's strength and beauty. Her knees never wobbled under a heavy load, and her shoulders stayed straight back when she walked.

But the old lady sneered at her robust daughter, "You

are so young and strong you can show off for your new husband. But I am just as strong." The young girl ignored the old lady and continued to sew her husband's caribou-skin anorak.

One day while the daughter waited for Kivioq to come home, the old lady sneaked up behind her and hit her on the head with a rock. Then, the jealous old woman stripped her daughter of her beautiful young skin and stepped into it herself. The new young skin covered the old woman's wrinkled face, bony arms and hands, and torso, but it would not stretch all the way down to her feet. Still, she was pleased with her new appearance, and she covered up the old skin of her legs with high boots.

Before long, Kivioq called from his kayak, and the old lady, disguised as his wife, slipped out the door to greet him. "You forgot to take off your boots," scolded Kivioq. But the old lady pretended she did not hear him and kept walking out toward the kayak. "Take off your boots," he protested again. "Boots do not belong in the water."

Finally the old lady took off the boots and threw them on the shore. After she reached Kivioq's kayak she grabbed hold of the caribou, just as her daughter had always done, and hoisted it onto her shoulder. But the animal's weight made her shoulders bend forward and her knees buckle. Kivioq thought his wife must be very tired.

He watched closely as his wife struggled to walk toward shore. Then he looked down in the water and saw two thin wrinkled legs below the fine young skin of his wife. Immediately, Kivioq understood his jealous mother-in-law's terrible deed.

"You cruel old woman. You have taken my wife from me," he shouted. And he turned his kayak around and paddled off in the opposite direction.

Kivioq never looked behind him. And he never again saw the old she-wolf who was his mother-in-law.

QUESTIONS AND ANSWERS

Q: *Explain how Kivioq's mother avenged his father's death.*

A: She taught Kivioq to resemble a seal who could lure the hunters out to sea. Then she used her powers to create a storm and killed them. Because Kivioq's mother did not know which hunter had killed her husband, she killed all of them.

Q: *What type of animal was Kivioq's spirit-protector, and what amulet did he carry?*

A: It was a small white bird called a snow bunting. Kivioq wore a string around his neck with a snow bunting's white feather attached to it.

Q: *What are three ways in which Kivioq's spirit-protector saved him from danger?*

A: Snow Bunting took Kivioq's clothing down from a line strung high above his head so he could escape the witch; he rescued Kivioq's canoe from two giant caterpillars who were trying to steal it; and he warned Kivioq before a huge clam could clasp him between its shells.

Q: *What did Kivioq discover when he finally arrived home?*

A: His mother was gone and his village was empty.

Q: *What did he do next?*

A: He mourned for his mother and his people, then set out to find a wife.

Q: *Who was the wife he found?*

A: Kivioq went to live with and finally married a she-wolf in human form.

Q: *What happened to Kivioq's wife?*

A: Her jealous mother killed her. Then the mother tried to disguise herself as the daughter to win Kivioq's affection.

Q: *How did Kivioq figure out that his mother-in-law had disguised herself as his wife?*

A: He noticed that the skin of his "wife's" legs was old and wrinkled beneath the boots she had taken off, and that she could not gracefully carry the weight of the caribou carcass.

Q: *What did Kivioq do next?*

A: He left his mother-in-law standing in the water. Eventually, she would die of starvation. He turned his kayak around and paddled away, never to return.

EXPERT COMMENTARY

Robert F. Spencer conducted ethnographic studies among the North Alaskan Eskimo in 1952 and 1953 with the support of the Arctic Institute of North America and the Office of Naval Research. He spent much of these years observing child-rearing practices and writes about some of them. Spencer's observations confirm the cultural correctness of Kivioq's mother's behavior in seeking vengeance for her husband's death and in training her son for this mission:

> There were for boys, however, certain rigors in the social environment. When the north wind blew, an infant boy might be placed outdoors for a time naked. This was felt to make the child hardy and to enable him to take his place as a man at a later time. . . Physical strength was prized.[3]
>
> But above all, defense of one's blood kin, vengeance for them, and responsibility for their actions were primary factors which served to affect family integration.[4]

Because the Netsilik world was inhabited by supernatural beings of many different kinds, amulets, or spirit-protectors, were carried by men, women, and children. The amulet either attached to the people's clothing or hung around the neck by a cord:

> . . . The physical appearance of the amulet was of little significance. The amulet received its supernatural power from the resident spirit exclusively and not because of any physical properties. Practically any small object could serve as an amulet.[5]

4

SEDNA, GODDESS OF THE SEA

BAFFINLAND INUIT OF NUNAVUT, CANADA

INTRODUCTION

The Inuit of Baffinland lived mostly on the southern two thirds of Baffin Island. This island is so large that in the southern portion, summer lasts longer than it does on the northern half. There are mountains in the north and along the southwestern coasts, flanked by low-lying plains, hills, lakes, plateaus, and valleys.

In winter, the Baffinland Inuit hunted seals, whales, and walruses, and during the summer and fall, they fished and hunted caribou. In April, men from several villages joined together and began a long trek inland over the mountains to follow the caribou herds. Only the hardiest men were invited to join the hunt, which required many days and many miles of walking. Hunters lived in skin-covered tents and moved with the migrating herds, which fed on the luxuriant crops of grey-green moss that pushed up through the melting snow. When hunting was especially good, men cached excess meat and hides in rocky caves and retrieved them later.

By early fall, Arctic char, a large type of salmon, began their annual migration to spawn upriver. Men built stone weirs along the mouths of rivers to catch as many fish as possible.

Seal hunting occupied much of the year in Baffinland, and a successful season depended on the whims of Sedna the sea goddess. Long ago, Sedna became the mother of the sea animals after her father cut off the joints of her fingers to save his life. As a powerful sea goddess, she could withhold the bounty of her animals whenever people broke taboos or otherwise made her angry. Then the local shaman had to be called upon to appease her. The shaman would go into a trance, and his mind would make a spiritual journey down to the bottom of the sea to visit the goddess. He would then comb dirt from her long hair until she was happy and relieved. After the shaman returned to his regular state of mine, Sedna would set the animals free again.[1]

Animals were so important to the Inuit of Baffinland that the local shaman could not afford to risk waiting until the animals became scarce. To appease the animals' spirit, he organized annual feasts in their honor. In spring, when seals could be found sunning themselves on the ice, the people held a festival to honor the seals. In fall, before the first caribou hunt, the people held a great festival to honor them. Full winter darkness marked the end of the yearly celebrations and the beginning of storytelling season.[2]

"Sedna, Goddess of the Sea" tells how sea animals were created. The story also reminds listeners that cowardly behavior is never acceptable: not only was Sedna's father made to drown for his cowardly act, but Sedna kept his soul imprisoned down under the sea so that it would never be free to become a spirit.

SEDNA, GODDESS OF THE SEA

A very long time ago, a young girl named Sedna lived with her widowed father in a small sealskin tent along the coast of Baffin Island. Sedna, who was beautiful, smart, independent, and willful, wanted a husband who was her equal. In fact, she was so particular that she turned down every suitor who came to visit. Sedna's father, Kinuk, did not mind that his daughter was so fussy because he loved her dearly and did not want to lose her.

One day, a long, sleek kayak carrying a handsome young man pulled up along the shore. Sedna asked her father if he recognized the style of the young man's clothing. "I have never seen an anorak with such beautiful black-and-white stripes," she said to her father.

"It is most unusual," he agreed. "And look at the stranger's spear. It is made of ivory." Although Sedna and her father were very curious about the young man, they remained hidden from view inside their little tent.

But the stranger cried out to Sedna: "Come to me. You will never be hungry, and you will live in a tent made of the most beautiful skins. You will rest on soft bearskins. Your lamp will always be filled with oil, your pot with meat."

Sedna pushed aside the thick caribou hide that

covered the front entrance of her tent and peeked out. "Oh," she gasped. "He is indeed handsome." But Sedna had a reputation to protect, and she could not run to the shore and join the handsome young man while the people of her village looked on. So she closed the tent flap and stood quietly.

The young man stepped out of his kayak, and, using the tip of his ivory spear, drew a picture in the sand. "This is the land to which I will take you," he said as he scratched a scene of rolling hills, fat animals, and large comfortable houses. "I have many furs to give you," he shouted. "And I will place necklaces of ivory around your neck."

Sedna stepped out from the door of the tent and in a shy voice asked, "Am I the only girl in the territory without a husband? Are there no other women to pursue than one who does not wish to marry?"

The young man's smiled broadened. "There are many women for such a rich man as myself. But I want only you."

Sedna was charmed. She had known handsome men before, but she had never been enchanted by their words. She went back indoors, filled a small sealskin pouch with her sewing needles, and walked slowly down to the shore. Sedna's father did not protest. He believed he could not have made a better choice himself. The old man smiled and waved goodbye to his beautiful daughter.

The handsome young man lifted Sedna gently into his kayak and turned quickly out to sea. That evening, their kayak stopped alongside a rocky coast backed by low rolling hills. There were no houses and no fat animals— just hundreds of loons.

Sedna stepped hesitantly out of the kayak and turned to ask her new husband the whereabouts of the beautiful home he had described, but when she turned around, she was being followed not by her husband, but by an elegant loon with black on his back and white on his breast and belly. "Oh," she cried. "I have run away with the spirit-bird!"

"I used my power to transform myself into a human after I fell in love with you," said the young loon. "Otherwise, you would not have come away with me."

Sedna cried inconsolably. She could not imagine living among a flock of loud birds, who waddled around on webbed feet, let alone marrying one. She begged and begged to be returned to her home. "Please," she said. "I will give you my bag of sewing needles, if you will let me go home. I will give you anything I own."

Her loon husband fluffed up the nest of loose plants he had made for her and ignored her pleas. He brought her dozens of fresh fish and fed her well. But still she begged to go home.

When Sedna had failed to return home, even to visit, her father set out to find her. The old man wandered for many days from one island to another in search of his daughter. At last he spotted the long sleek kayak that belonged to the handsome suitor, and he went ashore. The father was puzzled: there were no houses on the island, just hundreds of black and white loons. He called out his daughter's name, "Sedna. Sedna. Where are you?"

But he was answered only by the cry of the loons. Then he looked up and saw his once-beautiful daughter sitting on a nest sobbing. "Oh, my child. I will take you home." He took her in his arms, carried her to his kayak, and they paddled away as quickly as possible.

When Sedna's husband came home, he asked the other birds, "Where is my wife?"

"Her father came and took her away," they cried.

Quickly, Loon-Husband turned back into a human, jumped into his sleek kayak, and gave chase.

Sedna's father saw the young husband approaching in his kayak, and he hid Sedna underneath a pile of furs. "Where is my wife? I want to see her," demanded her husband. The old man ignored him and paddled on.

Sedna's husband suddenly grew very angry and whirled his paddle madly in the air. Then he struck the water with his paddle, first on one side of the boat and then the other. His head and body gyrated back and forth in the tight little kayak, and water splashed all around him. Suddenly, the young man's handsome anorak turned back into shiny black and white feathers, and the spirit-bird rose up out of his kayak. As the great bird flapped its wings, the strange, wild cry of the loon filled the air.

Within moments, a furious storm rose up out of the sea, and giant waves smacked against the little kayak where Sedna still hid under a cover of heavy furs. Although Sedna's father wanted to save his beautiful daughter, he was consumed with fear. The spirit-bird was seeking revenge, and the old man knew he must appease the angry spirit. There was only one way to satisfy the spirit-bird, and that was to throw his daughter overboard. Once her father had made this horrible sacrifice, Sedna struggled to keep her head above the water as giant waves washed over her. When at last she was able to grip the gunwales of her father's kayak, he was seized with fear, and cut away her half-frozen fingers. "I must," he cried, steeling himself against his own agony. "The spirit-bird makes the sea angry and demands your life."

Sedna's body slowly disappeared beneath the icy waters, and her grieving father returned home. The old man lay down on a thick pile of caribou hides inside the little tent he and Sedna had shared for so many years, and wept.

During the night, another storm filled the sea with giant waves. This time, the waves washed far up on shore and lashed against the little tent where Sedna's father lay sleeping. When the last wave returned to the sea that night, it took the old man with it, down to Sedna's home at the bottom of the sea.

Sedna glared at her father with a single large, hollow eye that shone like a winter moon on her defiant face—the other eye had been lost in the storm at sea. Her father recognized the thick black braids that hung down his

daughter's back, but the youthful beauty he had known had been replaced by the proud face of a great spirit-goddess.

Sea animals had been created from the joints of Sedna's severed hands: the first joint of her fingers became the seals of the sea; the second joint the whales of the sea; and the third joint the walruses of the sea. When Sedna was in a good mood, she made the animals plentiful, and no one went hungry.

Sedna protected the animals she had created from her dismembered fingers and reigned over a vast region where human souls, including her father's, were imprisoned as punishment after death.

QUESTIONS AND ANSWERS

Q: *What are the two major climate areas on Baffin Island?*

A: Baffin Island is so large that its northern section displays the harshest Arctic weather, while its southern section has the mildest Arctic weather.

Q: *Explain why Sedna went away with the young man in the black-and-white anorak.*

A: He was handsome and charming, and he promised her wealth and jewels and life in a beautiful land.

Q: *Who did Sedna's suitor turn out to be?*

A: The Inuit spirit-bird, which was a loon.

Q: *Why was Sedna unhappy?*

A: She cried to be free and return to her people, but the loon kept her in a nest on the cliffs.

Q: *Why did Sedna's father sacrifice his daughter's life?*

A: He feared the sea god, who demanded the girl's life, so he threw her overboard.

Q: *What happened to Sedna's fingers after her father cut them off?*

A: The first joint of her fingers became the seals of the sea, the second joint the whales of the sea, and the third joint the walruses of the sea.

Q: *What became of Sedna?*

A: She became the sea goddess. She went to live at the bottom of the sea and there commanded all the sea animals. She reigned over a vast region where souls, including her father's, were imprisoned after death.

EXPERT COMMENTARY

Julian W. Bilby, a fellow of the Royal Geographical Society, lived among the Inuit in Baffinland for twelve years during the early part of the twentieth century. In addition to describing their ways of living and hunting, and their customs and beliefs, Bilby recorded many of their legends. About the legend of Sedna, the sea goddess, Bilby said:

> The Sedna legend—a religious legend around which turns a large volume of Eskimo superstition—has its repulsive as well as its poetic aspects. . . . Belief in this legend, in the existence and the power of Sedna, a maleficent [evil] sea-goddess of the underworld, forms a large part of the Eskimo religion, and the annual autumnal festival arising out of it is the principal celebration in their calendar.[3]
>
> The sea creatures who owe their origin to Sedna belong to her and she controls them. She protects them, and causes the storms which bring wreckage and famine to the kayakers and sealers. Hence she is in Eskimo inimical [reflecting hostility] to mankind, the source of the worst evils they know, a spirit who has to be propitiated or quelled [brought to an end forcibly] by ceremony, as the case may be.[4]

5

OOGOON'S ADVENTURES ON THE KOBUK RIVER

THE INUIT OF KOTZEBUE SOUND, ALASKA

INTRODUCTION

The Kotzebue region of Alaska extends along the northern coast, from Cape Thompson in the north to Cape Espenberg in the south, and inland to the headwaters of three great rivers, the Kobuk, Noatak, and Selic, which empty into the sea at Kotzebue Sound. Arctic winters are long and cold in the region, but, for an area this far north, food sources are rich and varied. High rugged mountains run between the upper Noatak and Kobuk rivers and are approached by flat level plains where caribou, mountain sheep, and bears come to feed on lush crops of moss, grass, sedge, and lichen. Even in the higher elevations, willow and alder bushes grow along the rivers and streams, providing shelter for wolves, white foxes, wolverines, lynxes, and ermines. Spruce trees grow along valley floors and river banks.

The Inuit of the region did not build snow houses or hunt out on the frozen sea ice in winter. Strong water currents along the coast keep the Arctic waters churning all year, which make the ice very unstable. They did, however, hunt whales in open water along the coast during spring and summer.

Although much of the region suffers from long cold winters and short cool summers, inland temperatures in summer often go above 90 degrees Fahrenheit. Kotzebue Sound cuts deep into the land, and families often lived so far inland they only visited the coast in the summer during whaling season. This was the time of year when many different groups gathered to socialize, hold athletic competitions, play games, and feast.

In winter, families lived in large houses that were dug three to four feet into the ground. A plentiful supply of wood in the region allowed them to frame the walls that stood above the ground, and to cover the roofs of the houses with closely-placed wooden posts. Sod, grass, and moss were stacked on top of the posts to keep the houses warm. Most houses had a broad wooden platform running along the back interior wall of the house that was used for sleeping and sitting. Men hunted in kayaks and families moved about in large umiaks.[1]

"Oogoon's Adventures on the Kobuk River" is about a young man who lived so far inland that he had never seen the ocean. One day, however he paddled down the Kobuk River to the sea. During these adventures, Oogoon was protected by his amulet, an ermine crown that the young man wore on his head. Oogoon's parents, like all Inuit, fought to protect the souls of their children. If a child were to meet an untimely death far from home, his or her soul might be left to wander.[2]

OOGOON'S ADVENTURES ON THE KOBUK RIVER

By the time Oogoon was born, his parents were already old and living all alone far up along the Kobuk River. Oogoon had many brothers, but they had all left home as soon as they had reached manhood, and none of them had ever returned. Oogoon's parents would never know if their boys had met untimely deaths and, if they had, whether their souls might be wandering around lost. They feared the same fate might befall their youngest son.

So, to avoid such a fate for Oogoon, his parents catered to their son's every whim in the hope that he would never leave them. His mother fed him *au-goo-took*, an Inuit version of ice cream, and his father made him a furry crown of ermine to wear on his head. "This will be your spirit-protector," he said to his young son. "Amulets like this hold magical power and will keep you safe."

In summer, Oogoon chased squirrels among the thick spruce trees that grew along the river, and in winter he hunted for white fox, wolverines, and lynx with his father out on the frozen tundra.

As the years went by, Oogoon grew tall and strong. But his father could not tell if he had reached manhood. One day in early summer, Oogoon's father gave his son a strong new hunting spear made for a man. "It is time for you to hunt alone," said Oogoon's father.

Oogoon rubbed his fingers along the finely polished wooden spear-handle and then against the sharp stone blade his father had attached to the end. "It is a fine weapon," said Oogoon to his father. "I will make you proud."

Oogoon rose early the next morning and bounded down the path through the spruce trees in search of game. Even though he had traveled this way many times before with his father, it was the first time he had carried a spear and had been all alone. That evening, Oogoon returned home wearing a big smile and dragging a bird, a young ptarmigan.

When Oogoon's father saw the bird he heaved a sigh of relief. Oogoon had snared the ptarmigan, but it was obvious that he had not used his new spear. Even young children could snare birds, but it took the confidence and skill of a mature man to use a spear. The old man thanked the earth that his son was still a boy and would be likely to remain at home.

Before long, Oogoon's father inquired if he would like to go hunting again. "Yes," said Oogoon, "I had great success once before."

That evening Oogoon returned home with a small rabbit. He had snared the animal again, but had not used his new spear. Once more, the old man sighed, and thanked the earth that his son was still a boy.

Winter passed, and in spring Oogoon announced that it was time for him to go hunting again. When he returned home that evening, he dragged behind him a large caribou. This time it was clear that the animal had been felled by Oogoon's new spear, and this time his father did not give thanks to the earth. Instead, he made plans to kill his son before he could leave home.

The following morning, after Oogoon had left to go hunting, his father buried sharp spears beneath the snow along the trail Oogoon followed home. Then he hid behind a tall spruce tree and waited. At last, Oogoon came down the trail dragging two caribou. But when he saw the piles of disturbed snow along the trail, he swished his feet back and forth in the snow and uncovered the sharp spears his father had planted. Oogoon pulled up the spears, threw them aside, and continued on his way home as if nothing had happened. He did not mention the incident when the family ate together that evening.

The next morning Oogoon's father set a noose, a loop of rope used to hang people, above the door and waited to drop it on his son when he entered the house. But Oogoon's father did not hear his son approaching, and when the young man opened the door, the noose fell on the floor too soon. Oogoon stepped over the noose, and sat down to eat.

"Have you forgotten, father?" said Oogoon. "You can never succeed in killing me as long as I wear my ermine crown."

The old man hung his head in shame. "You are right," he said. "I will stop trying." So, Oogoon's parents forgot their fear of losing their son, and the family lived happily together for two more winters. Then, one cold spring morning Oogoon approached his father with a request: "I would like very much to have a kayak of my own. Will you make one for me?"

Oogoon's father knew that if he made his son a kayak, he would leave. Nevertheless, the old man made Oogoon a sturdy little craft and a long wooden paddle. When he had finished, he showed his son the sleek little boat and said, "Many of our people live far away where the river meets the sea. Perhaps you will find your brothers there."

When Oogoon was ready to leave, he placed the ermine crown on his head and tucked a bag of *au-goo-took* into the kayak. "Take a taste of au-goo-took whenever you sense danger," said his mother. "It will warn you if there is trouble."

Oogoon thanked his parents, stepped into his sleek new kayak, and disappeared down the swift waters of the Kobuk River. He paddled for many hours, content with the sound of water splashing softly against his shiny new paddle. Before long, Oogoon saw an old woman on shore, but she ran into the house when she saw him approaching. Oogoon remembered his bag of *au-goo-took* and quickly stuck his finger into the bag to take a taste. "There is danger here," said a low voice.

Oogoon got out of his kayak, stroked his ermine crown, and walked toward the old woman's house. As soon as he entered the tunnel leading to the house, its entrance sealed up behind him. It was too dark inside for Oogoon to see, so he felt around the walls until his finger sank into a small opening. The opening was just large enough for an ermine to squeeze through, so Oogoon took off his crown, turned himself into an ermine, and squirmed through the hole.

Once outside, Oogoon became a man again. He put the ermine crown back on his head, climbed into his kayak, and paddled away.

The following evening Oogoon saw another house along the river. Quickly, he reached into his bag and tasted the *au-goo-took*. Again he heard a voice warning, "There is danger here."

Prepared for another uncomfortable experience, Oogoon walked toward the entrance of the house. An old woman came out and invited him to spend the night in her home. Tired and hungry, Oogoon accepted. The old woman introduced him to her young daughter who sat sewing. After they had eaten, the old lady made a place on the platform for Oogoon to sleep. Oogoon waited until he heard the old lady and her daughter snoring before he stepped quietly onto the floor. He crept over to where the young girl slept, cut off her hair, and replaced it with his ermine crown. After he had settled back on the platform, Oogoon piled the girl's hair on his own head and went to sleep.

The following morning, Oogoon peeked from under his caribou-skin blanket and saw the old lady get up and reach for her carving knife. She crept over to the ermine crown and cut off the head beneath it, mistaking it for the head of the stranger. Then she crawled back underneath her warm caribou-skin blankets and went back to sleep.

Oogoon waited until the old lady was snoring. Then he got up, took back his ermine crown, and ran out the passageway. But he had underestimated the old woman: the entrance was tightly sealed and he could not get out. Oogoon searched frantically until he found a small hole in the doorway. Again, he turned into an ermine and squeezed out through the hole. Once safe outside, he turned back into Oogoon, and ran toward the river. A huge black bear came roaring out of the house, calling in the voice of the old woman, "You have tricked me. I gave you food and a bed, and you tricked me!"

Oogoon jumped into his kayak and paddled away as fast as possible.

Oogoon traveled for several more days without seeing another house. Then early one afternoon he came upon Kotzebue Sound, where the river meets the sea. He crossed the bay and paddled until he saw houses. This time when he tasted his mother's *au-goo-took*, he heard no warning, so he went ashore. "Is there anyone here?" he called.

An old couple came forward from behind the house and greeted him. "Please," said the woman, "Come in and meet our daughter. We seldom have visitors."

Oogoon followed the couple inside. Standing beside a small oil lamp was the most beautiful girl Oogoon had ever seen. When she turned her head, strings of shiny cooper beads hanging from her ears picked up the light from the seal oil lamp and threw it like tiny sparks around the room. Her black hair was twisted into two long shiny braids that fell far down her back, and three fine black tattoo lines ran from underneath her lower lip to her chin. Oogoon smiled for the first time since he had left home.

The family welcomed Oogoon into their lives. The old man taught him to hunt seals and walruses along the coast and took him inland to hunt caribou. Before long, Oogoon married the couple's beautiful daughter.

But Oogoon and the old couple did not always understand each other because they spoke different dialects. Only the daughter understood both her husband and her parents, so she acted as a translator.

One day, when Oogoon was on his way out of the house, his father-in-law said something Oogoon did not understand. He said, "Do not go up on the mountain with two peaks. There are two ferocious dogs up there who will attack you!"

Oogoon turned to ask his wife what her father had said, but she had gone out.

Since he did not understand what his father-in-law had said, Oogoon went to the mountain with two peaks. That evening when he returned from hunting, he told the family about his encounter with two fierce dogs, which he had killed to save himself.

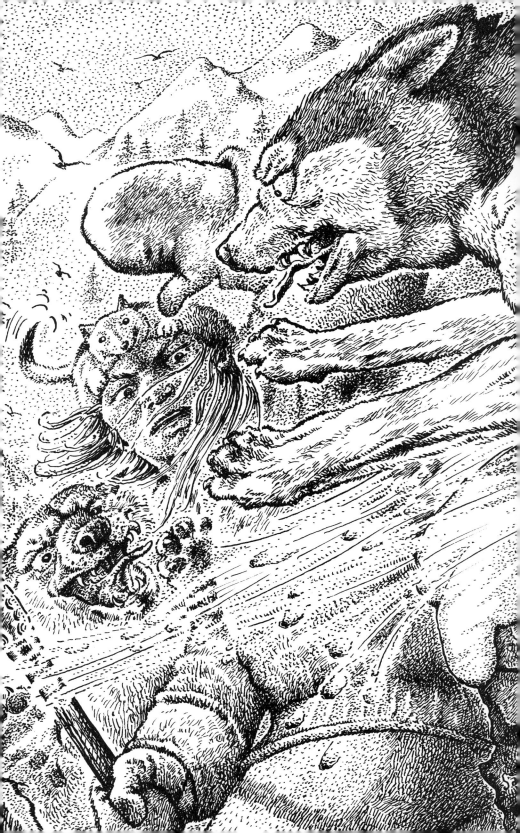

Quickly the old man hung his head in sorrow. "You have killed my sons! They were my hunters." The old man brooded for a long time. Then his sadness turned to anger, and Oogoon began to fear that the old man would seek revenge. Over the weeks that passed, Oogoon became very eager to please. Early one morning when the old man was leaving the house, he asked his son-in-law to make him a kayak.

"But there is no wood here," replied Oogoon. "I cannot make a kayak frame without wood."

"Go down to the shore where the waves bring forth wood from the sea. There you will find what you are looking for," answered the old man.

So Oogoon did what his father-in-law instructed and found a large log lying on the beach. He began to chop it up, but it was not dead wood, and it sprang back at him and almost killed him. Angry with his father-in-law for trying to trick him, Oogoon pounded at the log until it was too weak to spring back at him. The old man was surprised when Oogoon came home with enough wood to frame a kayak.

The following day, when Oogoon was resting in a small hunting shelter, his father-in-law poured oil down a hole in the roof and set the house on fire. Oogoon fought desperately to get out of the little house, but his father-in-law had sealed up the door. At last, Oogoon took off his ermine crown, turned himself into an ermine, and escaped through a tiny hole in the wall of the house. Once outside, he turned back into a man and sat down to rest.

Later, when Oogoon's father-in-law returned to view the young man's ashes, he found his son-in-law sitting calmly beside the burnt debris of the shelter. Neither man spoke as they walked home.

By the time summer arrived, Oogoon was a father. He was eager to take his wife and son to visit his parents far up the Kobuk River. So he packed his family into a small umiak, bade goodbye to his in-laws, and paddled across the bay.

However, just as Oogoon and his family approached the mouth of the river, a ferocious storm began to blow them in all directions. Their little boat bobbed up and down, rising and falling with great angry waves. Oogoon tried to turn back, but he could not steer the little boat. First his supplies flew overboard, then his baby son flew out of his wife's arms, and moments later the kayak tipped sideways and his beautiful wife disappeared into the water.

Oogoon held himself in the boat and fought desperately to stay afloat. After many hours, he managed to make his way back to the home of his in-laws. When he entered his old house, his beautiful wife sat sewing, and his young son lay sleeping beside her. Oogoon's father-in-law, surprised to see that he still had not succeeded in killing Oogoon, feared for his life and ran from the house.

The next day, Oogoon found his father-in-law resting in a hunting shelter. Oogoon sealed up the door with a huge boulder and poured oil inside through the roof, just as the old man had done to him. Then he set the shelter on fire.

Later, when Oogoon returned and found the charred bones of his father-in-law lying in the ashes, he knew he would not have to worry about his father-in-law's evil tricks any longer.

Oogoon took his wife and little son far up the Kobuk River to live with his parents. Oogoon's parents were delighted that at least one of their sons had returned home, and they would not have to worry that his soul might become lost. Oogoon's parents doted on their lovely daughter-in-law and spoiled their handsome young grandson, and they never tired of listening to their son's exciting adventures on the Kobuk River.

QUESTIONS AND ANSWERS

Q: *How did Inuit houses in the Kotzebue Sound region of Alaska differ from those in other parts of the Arctic?*

A: The Inuit of Kotzebue Sound did not live in igloos or hunt out on the sea ice in winter because water currents in the region made the ice too unstable. Instead, they dug houses three or four feet into the ground and built a frame and roof above the dugout portion. A plentiful supply of driftwood in the region gave them ample supplies for framing and roofing their houses, which they covered all over with sod.

Q: *Did Oogoon and his father hunt sea animals?*

A: No. They lived too far from the sea. They hunted caribou and smaller animals on the frozen tundra.

Q: *What was the amulet Oogoon's father made for him after he was born?*

A: A crown made from ermine fur.

Q: *How did Oogoon's father know when his son had become a man?*

A: The father could tell by the way his son had hunted his first caribou that Oogoon had used his new spear like a man.

Q: *Why did Oogoon's father want to kill his son?*

A: He feared Oogoon would leave home like his brothers and never return. If he killed his youngest son before he had a chance to leave home, Oogoon's father might be able to protect the boy's soul, should he be killed by an accident.

Q: *Whom did Oogoon meet first on his journey down the river?*

A: He met an old woman who lived along the shore.

Q: *How did Oogoon escape from the entrance to the woman's house?*

A: Oogoon called on his ermine spirit-helper, turned into an ermine, and squeezed out a small hole in the wall.

Q: *How did Oogoon protect himself in the house of the second old woman, who invited him to stay the night?*

A: When they all went to bed, Oogoon switched his ermine crown for the long hair of the old lady's young daughter, hoping to trick the old lady if she meant any harm.

Q: *What happened to the daughter?*

A: In the morning, the old lady crept out of bed and cut off the head with the ermine crown, believing she was killing the stranger instead of her daughter.

Q: *How did Oogoon find a wife?*

A: After he paddled down the Kobuk River he arrived in Kotzebue Sound where he visited a family along the shore. The family invited him to stay with them, and eventually Oogoon married their beautiful daughter.

Q: *Why did Oogoon's father-in-law try to kill him?*

A: The father-in-law had warned Oogoon not to go up into the mountain with two peaks. But Oogoon ignored the warning, went up the mountain, and killed two ferocious dogs there. They turned out to be his father in-law's sons.

Q: *Why did Oogoon ignore his father-in-law's warning?*

A: He did not understand the dialect spoken by his in-laws. Oogoon's wife had been his translator, and she had left the house before her father issued the warning.

Q: *How did Oogoon's father-in-law try to kill him?*

A: The father-in-law instructed Oogoon to make a kayak from driftwood, and the driftwood sprang up and tried to kill him. Then the old man tried to burn Oogoon by pouring hot oil down a hole in the roof of a hunting shelter in which the young man had stopped to rest.

Q: *What happened when Oogoon tried to take his wife and young son home to visit with his parents?*

A: His father-in-law, using magic, tried to have Oogoon killed in a storm at sea. Oogoon's son and wife who were swept overboard were saved and taken home. Oogoon surprised his father-in-law by surviving the ordeal and returning to his father-in-law's home to seek revenge.

Q: *Did Oogoon ever return to his own home?*

A: Oogoon killed his wicked father-in-law and returned home with his family to live with his parents on the Kobuk River.

EXPERT COMMENTARY

The Danish ethnologist Knud Rasmussen observed the use of amulets among groups in the Arctic and found that only on occasion were such amulets worn by women:

> Women rarely wore amulets on their own accord. The Eskimo idea is that it is the man and not the woman who has to fight the battle of life, and consequently, one finds little girls of five or six years old wearing amulets for protection of the sons they hope to bear–for the longer an amulet has been worn, the greater its power.[3]

Edward William Nelson, while doing field work for the Smithsonian Institution in Alaska during the late 1800s, collected many different types of amulets:

> Among the people of Kaviak Peninsula and Kotzebue Sound, a body of the common weasel [ermine], which is said to be one of the totem animals of the Eskimo, is very highly prized as a fetich [fetish: an object believed to possess magical power]. The body is dried entire and is worn on the belt or carried in a pouch by boys and young men. The possession of these weasel mummies is supposed to endow their owner with agility and prowess as hunters.[4]

Forty years ago, an Inuit author wrote *I Am Eskimo: Aknik my name*, in which he described various aspects of native life, including how to make Inuit ice cream:

> Mama Eskimo use reindeer or caribou fat for making ice cream. She took fat and chop it up fine. After chop it up, rounded it up again put it in a pan, and heat it a little. After she heat little she put seal oil and water on fine snow and start to work with hand and stir it up. Pretty soon that fat getting white and getting bigger and bigger. Pretty soon she have pan full of Eskimo ice cream.[5]

6

THE HILL GIANT
BERING STRAIT INUIT
OF ALASKA

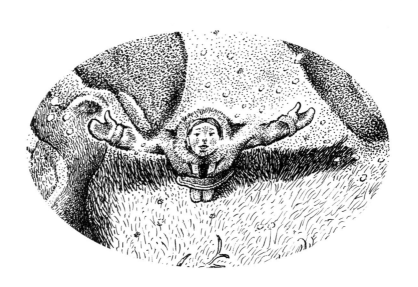

INTRODUCTION

The territory once occupied by the Bering Strait Inuit included the rocky, treeless islands in the strait. Offshore, it included most of the Seward Peninsula and the eastern shores of Norton Sound. The mountains on the mainland are flanked by miles of flat treeless tundra, and forty-nine square miles of the region lie north of the Arctic Circle. Sea ice forms in October and stays until June. Yet, the Inuit did not live or hunt out on the frozen ice in winter because the churning waters of the strait made the ice unstable and unsafe for travel.

Seals, whales, and walruses were hunted in spring and summer in open water. In June, fisherman caught coho, chum, and king salmon in local rivers. Women dried the salmon on driftwood racks at summer campsites. In July and August, women and children traveled up into the mountains to gather quantities of salmon berries, cranberries, and blueberries, which they also dried for winter.

In October, families returned from their inland summer fishing camps to their winter homes along the coast. Men dropped seal nets into the water to catch seals and hauled the nets in before the sea froze. Later, they put the nets into blow holes in the ice where the seals come to breathe.

Hunters corralled caribou on the mainland during the February and March migration season by driving them between a narrow row of large boulders or between two lines of men. Hunters waited at the end of the lines of men or rocks to spear the animals.

The Bering Strait Inuit dug large house foundations partially into the ground, framed them with tall posts, and covered them with sod, moss, and skins. In summer, these houses were entered by a ladder descending from the front door, and, in winter, by an underground tunnel leading up to the front door which was designed to keep out blowing wind, rain, and snow when entering and exiting the house.[1]

The wind that sweeps along the coast and islands near the Bering Strait is as fierce and cold as the wind that blows across the eastern Arctic. The story about "The Hill Giant," was a popular tale about the origin of severe weather. It was also a story about banishment, in which a young man was banished from his village by his own mother. In the Arctic, banishment was, in effect, a death sentence, since no one could survive in the region alone.

The mainland mountains of the region are formed by Kinak, the giant, who lay across the land covered with snow. It is undoubtedly Kinak who continues to breathe, sneeze, and cough severe wind and weather.[2]

THE HILL GIANT

Darkness covered the frozen tundra the night Taku slipped out the long underground entrance of the house she had shared for many years with her cruel young husband. Tired of being beaten, Taku was leaving and never coming back.

Taku pulled her caribou-skin anorak up around her face and headed west. She traveled for many days and nights, going out of her way to avoid houses and villages, fearing someone might see her and take her home. When she was sure all signs of human life were behind her, Taku slowed down.

Then, a cold wind began to whip her face, and she stopped to look for shelter. A series of large and small hills off in the distance gave her renewed energy, and she began to run toward them. At last Taku reached the smallest hill and made a clearing between two short ridges. She snuggled into the deep snow and fell sound asleep.

The following day, Taku continued to trek along the hills, and in the evening, she nestled down beside two small round hills. Each day, Taku climbed higher and higher along the hilly ridges until one morning a great booming voice awoke her: "Who are you? Humans never visit me. What are you doing here?"

Taku trembled with fright. She told the invisible voice her sad story and how she had been forced to run away from her husband's constant beatings.

"You may call me Kinak," said the voice. "My great body spreads out over the tundra, and I have allowed you to sleep between my toes and knees, on my chest, and now on my face. But you must never again sleep so close to my mouth or I will be forced to breathe on you and blow you away."

Taku trembled. "I did not realize I was traveling on the body of a giant," said the young wife. "I will leave right away."

The giant heaved a sigh. "You do not have to leave. Build a house in the thickest part of my beard, far away from my mouth. But go quickly. I must take a breath and clear my lungs right now."

Taku had barely settled in the giant's beard when a fierce wind roared out over the hills and heavy snow swirled across the tundra. While she waited for something more to happen, a dark cloud appeared in the sky and moved slowly toward her. When it was directly overhead, Taku recognized the outline of the giant's huge fist. The shadow lingered for a moment, then a freshly killed caribou dropped down beside her. Taku was so hungry she thanked the giant out loud. "Thank you. Thank you," she yelled into the sky. Taku quickly gathered hairs from the giant's beard, built a fire with the hairs, and ate heartily. She was pleased to be living with a giant who could stretch his arm toward the land and capture a caribou, or simply reach toward the sea and bring her seals and walruses.

Taku lived happily with the giant for many years. She ate well and fashioned fine clothing for herself from the many animals he brought. She had never been so happy and content.

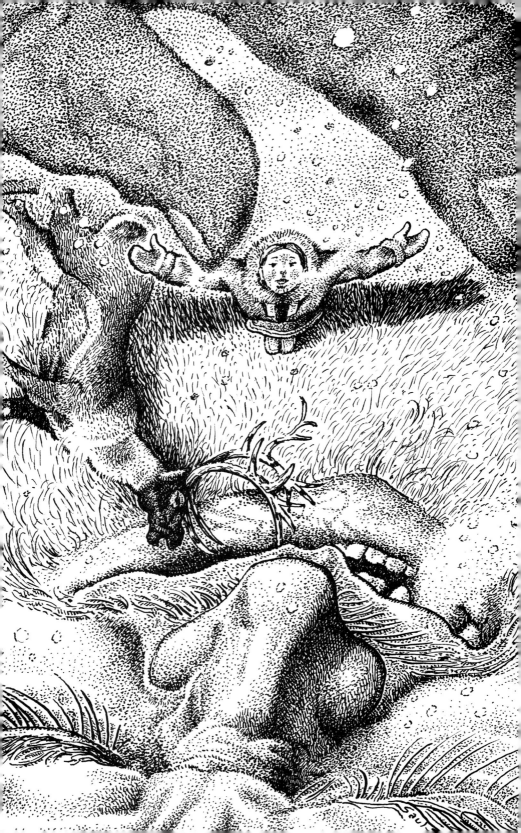

But one day, the giant called out to her. "Taku?" he asked. "Are you listening to me? I am tired of lying in one place. I must turn over. It is time for you to go home."

Taku trembled with fear. Her husband would surely inflict severe punishment on her for staying away so long. "I would like very much to go home," she said, "but I know my husband will beat me for staying away for so long."

"Do not worry," said Kinak. "I will protect you. If you are ever in danger, just call my name and I will come. But before you leave, you must cut both ears from each of the animal skins in storage and put them in a container to take home."

Taku did as she was told without asking Kinak for a reason.

"Now crouch down in front of my mouth and I will send you home," said Kinak.

Again, Taku did as she was told. The giant took a deep breath and WHOOSH, he expelled a powerfully strong wind that blew the young wife far out over the tundra. And before long, Taku landed in her old village. She walked slowly toward the house she had shared with her cruel husband, placed the container of animal ears in the storage shed outside the house, and went inside. To Taku's surprise, her husband greeted her with great joy. He told her he had mourned her death and believed he would never see her again. Taku's fears disappeared, and she settled back into her old household routines.

The next day, when Taku's husband went out to the storage shed, he found piles of fine well-tanned animal hides, one for every ear in Taku's container. The large quantity of fine furs would make Taku's husband a very rich man, and thus one of the village leaders.

Taku's husband was so pleased with his new status in the village that he forgot all about beating his wife.

Then one day Taku's husband told his wife he wanted a child. "What will become of us if we remain childless into our old age? Who will take care of us?" he argued. And that evening Taku's husband dipped a feather in oil and drew the form of a baby boy on his wife's abdomen.

Before long, Taku gave birth to a handsome little boy whom she named Kinak, in memory of the kind giant. Little Kinak soon grew up to be handsome and strong. But while her son was maturing into a fine young man, her husband was reverting back to his old ways. One day, Taku's husband got so angry when his food was not prepared on time that he picked up his spear and rushed toward her, intending to strike her.

Taku ran out of the house shouting, "Kinak. Kinak. Help!" Her husband, who believed she was calling their son, ignored her cries and chased her out through the long passageway.

Once outside, a fierce wind blew down from the north, picked up the angry husband, and whisked him off into the clear blue summer sky, never to be seen again.

Taku was pleased never to see her husband, and thrilled to have her young son all to herself. But young Kinak soon developed a cruel and fierce temper. Every day he bragged to his mother that he had killed a hunting companion. Often, the cocky young man boasted of having killed more than one.

"You are endangering both of our lives," Taku said to her son. "The families of your victims will seek revenge. They will kill both of us," she warned.

So Kinak behaved properly for some time thereafter, and nothing more was said about his evil deeds. Then, one day when he returned home from hunting, he told his mother he had killed his companion after a quarrel. Kinak's mother heaved a heavy sigh. "You are hated and feared in the village," she said at last. "Soon there will only be women and children living among us. It will be better for all of us if you go away and do not return."

Then Taku turned and walked away.

Some months later, after Kinak had filled his mother's storage racks with meat and skins, he said, "I have provided you with food and hides. Now I will go."

Kinak traveled north in the direction his mother had taken many years before. When he came upon the series of hills where his mother had lived for many years, he immediately climbed the highest one. No sooner had he reached the top when he heard the booming voice of the giant. "Who are you?" the giant asked the young man who was standing too close to his mouth. When Kinak the giant learned that the young man was the son of his friend Taku he smiled. "You may settle down on my face," said the giant. "But you must never climb onto my lips. If you do, evil will befall you."

Taku's son thanked the giant and settled down on his long wiry beard. But he was not accustomed to being told what to do, and soon he became restless. Finally, the bold young man decided to find out why the giant was so protective of his lips. It took a long time for the young man to make his way through the giant's thick tangled beard, but eventually he landed on the cleft of Kinak's deep chin. After he had caught his breath, Taku's son stepped up onto the giant's lower lip and looked over the edge. WHOOSH. A blast of ice-cold air whirled up out of the opening, picked up the surprised young man, and hurled him into the air. Round and round he spun until, eventually, he disappeared off into space.

Taku and her son were the last humans to visit the hill giant. But Kinak the giant still lives in the north and breathes out fierce winds and snow in winter to remind the people of his presence.

QUESTIONS AND ANSWERS

Q: *Describe the winter homes used by the Inuit of the region.*

A: They lived in large houses that were dug partially into the ground, framed above ground with wood, and covered with sod, moss, and skins. In summer, houses were entered by climbing down a ladder from the front door, and, in winter, through a long passageway dug below ground that kept blowing snow and wind out of the house when people entered and exited the doorway.

Q: *Identify five sources of food in the region.*

A: Several species of salmon spawned up local rivers in June and were quite plentiful. Cranberries, salmon berries and blueberries grew inland in summer, and seals were plentiful along the coast.

Q: *Why did Taku leave her husband?*

A: He was cruel and abusive.

Q: *In what direction did Taku go when she left home? And where was she when she met the hill giant?*

A: Taku walked north, but she had to seek shelter in the hills when a storm came upon her. She did not realize the hills upon which she settled were the toes, knees, chest, and face of a giant.

Q: *How did Taku's husband respond when she returned home?*

A: He was pleased to see her and welcomed her.

Q: *Why did Taku's husband become happier still?*

A: He discovered Taku's supply of animal hides. There were so many that her husband was now a wealthy man and enjoyed new prestige in his village.

Q: *What did Taku name her first young son?*

A: She named him Kinak, after her friend, the giant.

Q: *Describe the character of Taku's son.*

A: Taku's son grew up to be quick-tempered.

Q: *Why did Taku banish her son from their home and village?*

A: Because her son often murdered his hunting companions for no reason and Taku feared their families would seek revenge.

Q: *Where did Kinak go after his mother banished him?*

A: Kinak, the son, went into the hills where he unknowingly climbed on Kinak, the giant. Because the giant had fond memories of Taku, he allowed the young man to live on the side of his face.

Q: *What warning did the hill giant give to Taku's son?*

A: Kinak warned the young man never to climb up onto his lips.

Q: *Why did Kinak disobey the giant?*

A: He was not accustomed to being told what to do, and he was curious.

Q: *What happened to Taku's son?*

A: He disobeyed the giant, climbed onto his lower lip, and peered over the edge. The hill giant let out a great breath and sent Taku's son off into the sky forever.

EXPERT COMMENTARY

In his book *Race, Language and Culture*, Franz Boas includes a chapter on the folklore of the Eskimo. He describes what the Eskimos spoke of when they spoke of giants such as Kinak, as well as elves:

> There are giants of such size that they scoop up hunters and their boats in the hollow of their hands. Their boots are so large that a man can hide in the eyelet through which the shoe lacing is drawn. In tales of marriages between giants and man the incongruity of their sizes forms the subjects of coarse jokes.[3]

In the same book, Franz Boas also discusses men like Taku's son who kill other men for no apparent reason or for trivial reasons:

> A peculiar trait of Eskimo tales is the sudden springing up of hatred between men who had been the best of friends, which results in treacherous attempts on life. The causes for this sudden change from love to hatred are often most trifling. In one of the stories quoted here [*Race, Language and Culture*] the reason given is the failure of one of the friends to come back from the interior in season to take his share of the seals caught by his friend. In the second story the reason is that one man shoots the dog of another on being requested to do so. In the third, no reason whatever is given.[4]

7

OL-AN-UK
THE ORPHAN
ALEUTS, OR UNANGAN,
OF ALASKA

INTRODUCTION

The Aleut, or Unangan, people of Alaska are most often grouped with the Inuit of the region, even though their culture and language are very different.

The Aleut adapted to life on a string of treeless volcanic islands that stretch and curl like a long finger from the Alaska peninsula far out into the Pacific Ocean. For thousands of years they have fished and hunted whales, sea lions, and otters in one of the windiest regions in the world, where daily rain and fog are whipped up by icy winds that come down from the Bering Strait and collide with warm air moving northward with the Japan Current. The shallow waters in the straits and the deep waters of the Aleutian Trench that run between the tip of the islands and Russia create severe tides, riptides, and very dense fog. Aleut fishermen learned to navigate by the direction of the currents, and traveled through fog and darkness by "feeling" the direction of wind and water.

The Aleut built winter settlements near plentiful sources of fresh water and driftwood, and near tall cliffs from which men could look out to the sea for migrating whales. They dug their house foundations into the ground, framed them with driftwood posts, and covered the outsides with grass and sod. The irregular landscape of the islands made these homes hard to distinguish from the rest of the land.

Mild year-round temperatures, which range from 30 to 50 degrees Fahrenheit, a lack of permafrost, and rich volcanic soils nourished the growth of various grasses as well as cranberries, crowberries, lilies, and cowslip on the islands.

The Aleut have long been skilled kayakers and have

hunted whales in the rough waters surrounding the islands for thousands of years. Unlike other Arctic whale hunters, the Aleut used harpoons coated with a poison made from a plant belonging to the buttercup family, called aconite. After harpooning a whale, the Aleut would wait several days for the whale to die from the poison; then they would retrieve the floating carcass. Villagers kept track of the whereabouts of wounded animals and went out to haul them ashore after they died.[1]

The story of Ol-an-uk may be associated with festivals held at the beginning and end of the whaling season, during which the Aleut held competitions and sponsored contests to test men's strength and agility. Because Ol-an-uk was an orphan, he was unfamiliar with the traditional athletic competitions, but he rose to the challenge and proved himself stronger than a mature village champion.[2]

Ol-an-uk
the Orphan

Ol-an-uk lived alone on a small island where the wind blew day and night all year long. On the day that his parents did not return home in the evening, Ol-an-uk went down to the shore. His parents, their tools, and fishing nets had all been swept out to sea and vanished without a trace.

Ol-an-uk mourned the loss of his parents throughout the long winter. In spring, he walked aimlessly along the rocky shore tossing rocks into the water and calling out to the whales. "Come," he called. "It is spring and I am hungry." But Ol-an-uk knew that the whales would not come to him. He would have to muster the courage to go out into the fog-enshrouded sea and hunt the great beluga, or white, whales that had already begun to migrate north. But now, without his father, the excitement of chasing a pod of beluga whales was gone. He would really have to force himself to go hunting.

The day Ol-an-uk set out to hunt, the wind blew fog and mist in circles around his sturdy kayak. He paddled hard around the tiny island and out into the current. He would not be able to see the whales through the fog. Instead, he would have to detect their presence by listening as they splashed rhythmically through the water. At last, Ol-an-uk heard their sound and paddled quickly in their direction. He grabbed his harpoon in one hand, and with the other hand he maneuvered the kayak until he was gliding silently beside a young beluga. He raised his harpoon into the air and threw it with all his might. The young whale stopped just long enough for Ol-an-uk to know he had made a direct hit. His father would have been proud.

The years passed, and soon Ol-an-uk became a young man in need of a wife. One day, when the wind slept and the sea rested, Ol-an-uk filled a small sealskin pouch with seal oil. He would use it to flavor dried roots and unpalatable fish in case he had trouble finding fresh food. Ol-an-uk tucked the pouch of oil into his kayak and left his island.

Suddenly, a strong current pulled him out into the swiftly running water. Ol-an-uk paddled furiously to break the current's grip: first on one side of the little boat, then on the other. He held his head high to determine the wind direction, and sat perfectly still to feel the current. Ol-an-uk's strong even paddle strokes kept him balanced and upright, even though he did not know where the current would take him.

At last, Ol-an-uk saw the outline of an island through the fog and paddled hard to break free from the fast-moving current. He headed toward a large grassy swelling that appeared to be a dugout house rising above the rocks at the south end of the island. As he pulled his kayak up onto the shore, a beautiful young girl came down to greet him. She had smiling brown eyes and three perfectly spaced lines tattooed on her chin.

"You are a stranger," she said smiling. "Why have you come?"

Ol-an-uk stammered. "I, I, I, was lonely."

"You will not be lonely here. We have many families on the island. They are up in the meadow playing games before it is time to go whale hunting." The beautiful young girl turned and walked toward the house, "Come. I will feed you," she said.

Before long, the local chieftain, hearing that a stranger was among them, came to the young girl's house and invited Ol-an-uk to compete in the village games. "Samik, our village champion, is eager for a new challenge," said the chief. "Please come."

The young girl was not fond of Samik and wished to see him beaten. "You must accept the challenge, Ol-an-uk," she said. "It is our custom. Besides, you are stronger and more clever than he," she said with a sly smile.

Reluctantly, Ol-an-uk went with the chief to meet the village champion. Their first contest was to hunt for a beluga. Ol-an-uk smiled as he stepped confidently into his long thin kayak. He was already an expert whale hunter. After he and the village champion had lined up their kayaks side by side, the chief rested a bow and arrow on the gunwales between them. "The winner is to use this on the man who loses," he said.

Ol-an-uk paddled cautiously behind Samik who seemed to know in which direction to paddle to find whales. But the two hunters had barely lost sight of shore when high waves in the open sea began to toss their kayaks from side to side. Ol-an-uk tried desperately to keep his opponent in sight. But the familiar silence of fog and the strong water current in which Ol-an-uk was used to hunting whales had been replaced by blowing winds, wet heavy mist, and tall waves. Ol-an-uk struggled for many hours to keep himself afloat in the angry sea, but eventually he had to turn around and go back to the island defeated. His skin beneath the waterproof anorak turned cold at the thought of facing Samik who would be waiting for him on shore ready to use the victor's bow and arrow. Slowly, Ol-an-uk paddled toward the island. He wanted only to see the beautiful young girl with brown eyes one more time before he died.

But when Ol-an-uk arrived on shore, only Samik's kayak rested on the rocky shore. Ol-an-uk walked slowly through the thick silence toward the house of his beautiful hostess. "Do not be afraid," she said cheerfully as she stepped out of the door. "Samik did not harpoon a whale, either. He has gone inside to sulk."

Several days later, the village chief asked Ol-an-uk to compete in a kayak race with Samik. They were to race their kayaks around a large island just offshore. The first one around the island and home again would be the winner. Villagers came down to the shore to watch the two young men start out. At first the race was very exciting. The village champion took the lead, and cheers rose up from his friends on shore. But when Ol-an-uk passed Samik, the cheering on shore died down. Eventually, Samik paddled faster and faster until he left Ol-an-uk far behind him. Villagers clapped and cheered for their kinsman, all except the beautiful young girl with smiling brown eyes who wanted Ol-an-uk to win.

Before long, Ol-an-uk fell so far behind Samik that the villagers lost interest in the race and went home. Ol-an-uk realized it was time to talk to his little beluga-skin boat. "Become a beluga whale," he said to the little boat. "And swim fast."

Then the beluga whale dove under the water, passed beneath Samik's kayak, and swam swiftly toward shore. As the whale approached the island, it rose to the surface and assumed the form of the young man, Ol-an-uk.

In the meantime, Samik paddled leisurely toward

shore, confident that he had left the young stranger far behind. But when he finally arrived home, Ol-an-uk was waiting for him on the shore with his spear raised above his head. As Samik stepped out of his kayak, Ol-an-uk hurled the spear at the cocky young man and killed him.

This time, the villagers did not cheer, and the beautiful young girl covered the broad smile on her face with both hands. That evening when Ol-an-uk and the young girl were eating, the chief came to their door. "We cannot remove your spear from the body of Samik," he said. "Will you come down to the shore and remove it?"

Ol-an-uk followed the chief out of the house and down to the shore. But as soon as Ol-an-uk removed his spear from Samik's chest, the village champion smiled, stood up, and walked away.

The next day, the chief returned once again. "Samik, our village champion, challenges you to a wrestling match."

Ol-an-uk was growing tired of his cocky competitor's challenges and regretted having removed his spear from Samik's chest. But he did not want to disappoint his hostess and accepted the challenge.

Ol-an-uk followed the chief to a large house that had an indoor pit filled with black worms that squirmed among piles of old bones. "You must wrestle until one of you throws the other into the pit to be eaten by the worms," said the chief.

Ol-an-uk's arms were strong from paddling against the tough currents around his small island. This time he was confident he would compete for the last time with the cocky village champion. But as they began to wrestle, Samik caught Ol-an-uk off guard and quickly pinned his arms behind his back. Ol-an-uk struggled until he got a foot between Samik's legs. Then he curled it around one of

Samik's legs and pried himself loose. Quickly, Ol-an-uk got behind the village champion and wrapped his strong arms around Samik's chest. The village champion tried desperately to wrench himself free, but Ol-an-uk had pinned his arms to his sides leaving only his feet free. Samik twisted first one leg and then the other around and between Ol-an-uk's legs but could not throw him off balance. Slowly, Ol-an-uk began to squeeze the cockiness out of Samik's broad chest. He squeezed and squeezed while Samik gasped for breath and pleaded to be released. When Ol-an-uk could feel that Samik was totally limp, he shoved him face-down onto the ground. Before Samik could catch his breath, Ol-an-uk picked him up by the seat of his pants and collar, lifted him into the air, and hurled him into the worm pit.

At last, the villagers cheered for the young stranger. "You are indeed a true champion," said the village chief to Ol-an-uk. "Now you may claim the spoils of your victory: Samik's two wives, many fine weapons, and a storage room filled with meat."

Ol-an-uk accepted his victory prizes and returned to the house of the beautiful brown-eyed girl. "Will you come home with me?" he asked. "I have won two wives who will do all the work around our home. You shall be my traveling companion."

The beautiful young girl had already placed her belongings in a sealskin pouch and was ready to leave. "I will go with you," she said.

Thereafter, the young orphan boy, Ol-an-uk, was never alone again on his little island.

QUESTIONS AND ANSWERS

Q: *List two major differences between the Inuit and the Aleut.*

A: The Aleut speak a different language from their Inuit neighbors. Unlike the Inuit, the Aleut once owned slaves, had a strict class system, and recognized chieftains. The Inuit did not have an organized system that included chieftains. Instead, they recognized the best hunter or most accomplished medicine man as their leader.

Q: *Name the islands on which the Aleut live and the ocean that surrounds the islands.*

A: They live on a long chain of islands that stretch from the Alaska peninsula out into the Pacific Ocean, called the Aleutian Islands.

Q: *Is the weather on the Aleutian Islands typically Arctic?*

A: No. The warm waters of the Japan Current flow close to the islands and create mild year-round temperatures.

Q: *What happened to Ol-an-uk's parents?*

A: They were swept out to sea while they were repairing fishing nets on the shore.

Q: *What did Ol-an-uk eat to survive?*

A: He hunted great beluga whales.

Q: *Why did Ol-an-uk finally leave his island?*

A: He had grown into a man and wanted to find a wife.

EXPERT COMMENTARY

Edward William Nelson held a United States Army Signal Service post in St. Michael, Alaska in the late 1800s. Nelson, a naturalist, took the Army post because it included an arrangement with the Smithsonian Institution that allowed him to travel and collect data. The Smithsonian honored Nelson in 1983, on the one hundredth anniversary of his pioneering fieldwork.

Nelson observed many games and competitions among the Inuit:

> The men, each in his kaiak [kayak], are ranged side by side near the shore, and then at a signal paddle around a rock or islet, the winner being he who first touches the shore on returning to the starting point. . . . I heard of an instance where a white man visiting the village of the Malemut at Kotzebue Sound during the winter was repeatedly challenged to wrestle by one of the villagers. Finally, the annoyance became so great that the stranger accepted the challenge, and, being an extremely powerful man, seized the Eskimo and dashed him to the floor of the kashim [men's house], so heavily that he was badly hurt. This was considered quite legitimate and the stranger was not molested further.[3]

Nelson also collected thousands of artifacts, gathered a large number of animal specimens, and recorded many of the myths associated with the flora and fauna of Alaska. He wrote the following about worms:

> Ti'-sikh-puk, the great worm . . . which figures in numerous tales, was shaped like an enormous worm or caterpillar. It lived in the days when animals were supposed to have the power of changing their form at will to that of human beings, and in the tales it is indifferently a worm or a man. Among the carvings in ivory representing this creature were several having the body shaped like a worm with a human face on the head.[4]

⚛ GLOSSARY ⚛

Aleut (Unganan)—Descendants of a group of Arctic people who settled on the Aleutian Islands more than four thousand years ago. These people speak Aleut, a language different from that of the Inuit people.

amulet—A magical charm—a piece of animal hide, bone, teeth, or tusks—often worn as a necklace or belt, or sewn onto clothing to protect the wearer against harm.

Arctic—A huge area of land and water that includes three continents: North America, Asia, and Europe. The Arctic is the region of the world where trees cannot grow.

Arctic Circle—The imaginary line around the region of the North Pole that shows where the sunlight falls upon the Arctic when the earth is tilted toward the sun, and where there is no light at all when the earth is tilted away from the sun.

atliarusek—An Inuit word for elf or gnome.

auk—A black-footed bird with a heavy head, bull neck, and deep flattened bill with a white mark at its middle. These species breed from the Gulf of St. Lawrence area northward. No living great auk has been found since 1844, but the razorbill auk is still found in Greenland.

blubber—The layer of fat that lies beneath the skin of seals, whales, and walruses. Blubber was an important source of fuel and light in the Arctic.

breathing hole—Also called a "blow hole," an opening made in the ice by seals from underneath to provide breathing places in winter.

caribou—A large member of the deer family, which migrates from the northern regions of the Arctic in summer to the tree line in southern regions of the Arctic in winter (called reindeer in Europe).

ermine—A weasel with a valuable winter coat that is white in winter.

fjord—A long narrow inlet, or arm of the sea, bordered by steep rocky cliffs.

floe—A mass of thick ice; in the sea, a large or small single piece of floating ice.

gunwales—The sides or upper portions of a boat.

harpoon—A weapon with a long wooden handle and a pointed end made of bone, stone, or antler, used to kill sea animals.

igloo—A temporary winter house made out of blocks of snow. The word igloo was taken from the Inuit word for house, *iglu*.

Inuit—The people of the Arctic, formerly referred to as Eskimo. Inuit is also one of the languages of the Arctic people.

kayak—A long, slim, one-man boat framed with driftwood or whalebone and covered with sealskin. Hunters wear sealskin jackets that are attached to the round opening of the boat where the man sits. These jackets prevent water from getting into the boat if it rolls over in the water.

lichen—A combined fungus and microscopic green plant (alga) growing together. Lichen can grow in the absence of soil.

musk ox—A large animal related to goats and sheep that lives permanently in the Arctic and does not migrate.

narwhal—A type of whale that has a long tusk that extends from its lower jaw. In the male, the underside is all white.

permafrost—A permanent layer of frozen earth covered with ice and snow.

⚛ CHAPTER NOTES ⚛

Preface

1. *The Chronicle of Higher Education*, March 13, 1998 v44 n27 p22(2) <http://web7.infotrac.galegroup.com/itw/i...RCM_0_ A20421626&dyn=26!ar_fmt?sw_aep=sud> (July 21, 2000).

2. Knud Rasmussen, "The Intellectual Culture of the Iglulik Eskimos," *Report of the Fifth Thule Expedition—1921-24*, vol. 7, no. 1 (Denmark: Glydensdalske Boghonded, Nordisk Forlog, 1931), p. 62.

3. Knud Rasmussen, "The Netsilik Eskimos: Social Life and Spiritual Culture," *Report of the Fifth Thule Expedition—1921-24*, vol. 8, no. 1–2 (Denmark: Glydensdalske Boghonded, Nordisk Forlog, 1931), p. 209.

4. Wendell H. Oswalt, *Eskimos and Explorers* (Novato, Calif.: Chandler & Sharp Publishers, Inc., 1979), p. 184.

5. Knud Rasmussen, *Across Arctic America: Narrative of the Fifth Thule Expedition* (Fairbanks: University of Alaska Press, 1999), p. 81.

6. Ann Meekitjuk Hanson, *What's in a Name?* n.d., <www.nunavut.com/nunavut99/english/our.html> (March 13, 2000).

7. Rasmussen, *Across Arctic America: Narrative of the Fifth Thule Expedition*, p. 195.

8. Julian W. Bilby, *Among Unknown Eskimo* (London: Seeley Service & Co., Ltd, 1923), p. 185.

9. Oswalt, p. 51.

10. Norman Chance, *Arctic Circle* n.d., <http://borealis.lib .uconn.edu/ArcticCircle/HistoryCulture (December 1, 2000).

11. Inunit Circumpolar Conference, *President's Message* <http://www.inusiaat.com> (December 1, 2000).

12. Department of Indian Affairs and Northern Development <www.inac.gc.ca.> (November 17, 2000).

13. Ann Meekitjuk Hanson <www.nunavut.com/nunavut99/ english/our.html>

14. Peter Freuchen, *Book of the Eskimo* (Greenwich, Conn.: Fawcett Publications, Inc., 1961), pp. 178-189.

15. Hinrich Rink, *Tales and Traditions of the Eskimos* (Mineola, N.Y.: Dover Publications, Inc., 1997), p. 183.

16. Rasmussen, "The Netsilik Eskimos: Social Life and Spiritual Culture," pp. 365–379.

17. Bilby, pp. 187–195.

18. Edward Kiethahn, *Igloo Tales* (Washington, D.C.: Department of the Interior, 1944), pp. 48-55.

19. Edward William Nelson, *The Eskimo About Bering Strait* (Washington, D. C.: Smithsonian Institution Press, 1983), pp. 471–473.

20. Frank Albert Golder, "Eskimo and Aleut Stories from Alaska," *Journal of American Folklore 22* (1909), pp. 17–18.

21. Randburg, *Foreign Relations* <http:www.randburg.com/gr/general/general_17.html>, n.d.

22. The World Book Multimedia Encyclopedia (TM) © 1996 World Book, Inc. (Chicago, IL).

Chapter 1. The Woman Who Adopted a Bear

1. John Ross, *Voyage of Discovery, Made Under the Orders of the Admiralty, in his Majesty's Ships, Isabella and Alexander, for the Purpose of Exploring Baffin's Bay, and Inquiring into the Probability of a North-West Passage* (London: J. Murray, 1819), p. 89.

2. David Damas, ed., *Handbook of North American Indians*, vol. 5 (Arctic) (Washington, D.C.: Smithsonian Institution Press, 1984), pp. 577–594.

3. Peter Freuchen, *Book of the Eskimos* (Greenwich, Conn.: Fawcett Publications, Inc., 1961), pp. 178–189.

4. Knud Rasmussen, *Greenland by the Polar Sea: The Story of the Thule Expedition from Melville Bay to Cape Morris Jesup* (New York: AMS Press Inc., 1976), p. 12.

5. Knud Rasmussen, *The People of the Polar North* (New York: AMS Press, 1976), p. 123.

6. Knud Rasmussen, "The Netsilik Eskimos: Social Life and Spiritual Culture," *Report of the Fifth Thule Expedition—1921–24,* vol. 8, no. 1–2 (Denmark: Glydensdalske Boghonded, Nordisk Forlog, 1931), p. 139.

Chapter 2. The Girl Who Married a Gnome

1. David Damas, ed., *Handbook of North America Indians*, vol. 5 (Arctic) (Washington, D. C.: Smithsonian Institution Press, 1984), pp. 595–621.

2. Ibid., pp. 622–639.

3. Hinrich Rink, *Tales and Traditions of the Eskimo* (Mineola, N.Y.: Dover Publications, Inc., 1977), pp. 183–186.

4. Asen Balikci, *The Netsilik Eskimo* (Prospect Heights, Ill.: Waveland Press, Inc., 1970), p. 205.

5. Helge Ingstad, *Nunamiut: Among Alaska's Inland Eskimos* (New York: W. W. Norton & Company, Inc., 1954), p. 181.

Chapter 3. The Adventures of Kivioq

1. David Damas, ed., *Handbook of North America Indians*, vol. 5 (Arctic) (Washington, D. C.: Smithsonian Institution Press, 1984), pp. 415–430.

2. Knud Rasmussen, "The Netsilik Eskimos: Social Life and Spiritual Culture," *Report of the Fifth Thule Expedition—1921–24,* vol. 8, no. 1-2 (Denmark: Glydensdalske Boghonded, Nordisk Forlog, 1931), pp. 365-379.

3. Robert F. Spencer, *The North Alaskan Eskimo* (Washington, D. C.: United States Government Printing Office, 1959), p. 237.

4. Ibid., p. 75.

5. Asen Balikci, *The Netsilik Eskimo* (Prospect Heights, Ill.: Waveland Press, Inc., 1970), p. 201.

Chapter 4. Sedna, Goddess of the Sea

1. Julian W. Bilby, *Among Unknown Eskimo* (London: Seeley Service & Co. Ltd, 1923), pp. 187–195.

2. David Damas, ed., *Handbook of North American Indians*, vol. 5 (Arctic) (Washington, D. C.: Smithsonian Institution Press, 1984), pp. 463–475.

3. Bilby, pp. 184–185.

4. Ibid., p. 193.

Chapter 5. Oogoon's Adventures on the Kobuk River

1. David Damas, ed., *Handbook of North American Indians*, vol. 5 (Arctic) (Washington, D. C.: Smithsonian Institution Press, 1984), pp. 303–319.

2. Edward Kiethahn, *Igloo Tales* (Washington, D. C.: Department of the Interior, 1944), pp. 48–55.

3. Knud Rasmussen, *Across Arctic America: Narrative of the Fifth Thule Expedition* (Fairbanks: University of Alaska Press, 1999), p. 184.

4. Edward William Nelson, *The Eskimo About Bering Strait* (Washington, D. C.: Smithsonian Institution Press, 1983), p. 437.

5. Paul Green, *I am Eskimo: Aknik my name* (Bothwell, Wash.: Alaska Northwest Books, 1959), p. 79.

Chapter 6. The Hill Giant

1. David Damas, ed., *Handbook of North American Indians*, vol. 5 (Arctic) (Washington, D. C.: Smithsonian Institution Press, 1984), pp. 285–302.

2. Edward William Nelson, *The Eskimo About Bering Strait* (Washington, D.C.: Smithsonian Institution Press, 1983), pp. 471–473.

3. Franz Boas, *Race, Language and Culture* (Chicago, Ill.: The University of Chicago Press, 1982), p. 512.

4. Ibid., p. 513.

Chapter 7. Ol-an-uk the Orphan

1. David Damas, ed., *Handbook of North American Indians*, vol. 5 (Arctic) (Washington,D. C.: Smithsonian Institution Press, 1984), pp. 161–184.

2. Frank Albert Golder, "Eskimo and Aleut Stories from Alaska," *Journal of American Folklore 22* (1909), pp. 10–24.

3. Edward William Nelson, *The Eskimo About Bering Strait* (Washington, D. C.: Smithsonian Institution Press, 1983), p. 340.

4. Ibid., p. 443.

FURTHER READING

Bierhorst, John. *The Dancing Fox: Arctic Folktales*. New York: William Morrow and Company, Inc., 1997.

Bruchac, Joseph, ed. *Raven Tells Stories: An Anthology of Alaskan Native Writing*. Greenfield Center, New York: The Greenfield Review Press, 1991.

Finley, Carol. *Art of the Far North: Inuit Sculpture, Drawing, and Printmaking*. Minneapolis, Minn.: Lerner, 1998.

Lowenstein, Tom. *Ancient Land, Sacred Whale: The Inuit Hunt, Its Rituals and Poetry*. London, England: The Harvill Press (UK), 2000.

Oman, Lela K. *The Epic of Qayaq: The Longest Story Ever Told by My People*. Seattle, Washington: University of Washington Press, 1996.

Santella, Andrew. *The Inuit*. Conn.: Children's Press, 2001.

Seidelman, Harry and James Turner. *The Inuit Imagination: Arctic Myth and Sculpture*. New York: Thames & Hudson, 1994.

Von Finckenstein, Maria, ed. *Celebrating Inuit Art, 1948–1970*. Toronto, Ontario: Key Porter Books, 2000.

INTERNET ADDRESSES

Indian and Northern Affairs Canada—Publications

email: InfoPub@inac.gc.ca

Greenland

<http://www.greenland-guide.dk/gt/visit/green-10.htm>
<http://www.randburg.com/gr/general/general_8.html>
<http://www.greatestplaces.org/notes/g_land.htm>
<http://www.geogr.ku.dk/research/projects/articlan2.htm>

Canadian Arctic—Nunavut

<http://www.nunavut.com/home.html>
<http://www.arctic-travel.com/chapters/incultpage.html>

Alaska

<http://www.chevron.com/community/education/alaska/
student_act.html>
<http://www.mnh.si.edu/arctic/features/croads/aleut.html>
<http://borealis.lib.uconn.edu/ArcticCircle/HistoryCulture/
Aleut/Jones/ch1.html>

≋ INDEX ≋

A

Alaska, 6, 7, 8, 9, 10, 12, 13, 15, 16, 18, 79, 90, 107, 116, 117
Aleutian Islands, 15, 16, 18, 108, 116
Aleut people, 15, 18, 107–108, 116
American Indians, 8
amulets. *See* magic charms.
angatoks. *See* shamans.
Angudluk, 27, 28, 29, 30, 31, 32, 34, 38
anoraks, 11, 20, 54, 60, 63, 70, 73, 76, 97, 111
Arctic Circle, 6, 7, 95
Arctic Ocean, 6
Arouk, 45, 46, 47, 48, 49, 50, 51, 52, 53
Asia, 6
atliarusek. *See* gnomes.
au-goo-took, 81, 84, 85

B

Balikci, Asen, 54
Bering Strait, 6, 15, 95, 96, 107
Bliby, Julian W., 77
blubber, 11, 23, 27, 29, 50
Boas, Franz, 13, 105

C

Canada, 8, 10, 12, 13, 14, 15, 16, 17, 22, 56
caribou, 7, 9, 10, 11, 22, 49, 50, 54, 56–57, 62, 63, 65, 68, 69, 70, 73, 79, 82, 83, 86, 90, 93, 95, 97, 98
China, 6
clothing, 11–12
creation myths, 8
culture heroes, 9

D

dogsleds, 6, 11, 23, 27, 28, 30, 31, 32, 36

E

ermine, 18, 79, 80, 81, 83, 84, 85, 88, 90, 91, 93
Eskimo, the term, 6, 16, 17
Europe, 6

F

family life, 12
fjords, 32, 33, 36, 43, 45, 47, 48, 50

G

gnomes, 17, 44, 46, 47–48, 49, 50, 51, 52, 54
Greenland, 6, 7, 8, 10, 12, 13, 14, 15, 16, 17, 18, 22, 25, 40, 43, 44, 52

H

Hill Giant, the, 18, 96, 97–98, 100, 102, 103, 105

I

igloos, 10, 18, 23, 38, 43, 56
Ingstad, Helge, 54
Inuktitut. *See* Inupiak.
Ituko, 30, 31, 35, 36–37, 38
Inupiak, 13, 16, 40

K

kayaks, 11, 20, 22, 43–44, 45, 47, 48, 50, 58, 59, 62, 63, 65, 70, 71, 72, 73, 80, 83, 84, 85, 88, 92, 109, 110, 111, 112, 113, 117
Kinuk. *See* Sedna.
Kivioq, 17, 18, 57, 58–60, 62, 63, 64, 66
Kobuk River, 18, 79, 80, 81, 84, 89, 91, 92

L

loons, 71, 72, 73, 76

M

magic charms, 9, 14, 57, 64, 66, 80, 81, 83, 84, 85, 88, 90, 91, 93
magic words, 9
moon, 8, 22, 74
musk ox, 7, 11

N

narwhals, 22, 35
Nelson, Edward William, 93, 117
Netsilik people, 8, 54, 55–56, 66
North America, 6
North Pole, 22
Nunavut, 16, 54, 55

O

Ol-an-uk, 18, 108, 109–110, 111–112, 113, 115, 116
Oogoon, 18, 80, 81–83, 84–86, 88, 90, 91

P

Pacific Ocean, 15, 107, 116
parkas. *See* anoraks.
permafrost, 7, 107
polar bears, 7, 17, 18, 22, 32, 39
Polar Inuit, 22–23, 25, 38, 40, 43, 52

R

Rasmussen, Knud, 8, 10, 13, 17, 40–41, 93
Raven, 8, 9
Rink, Henry, 13
Ross, John, 22

S

Samik, 111, 112–113, 115
seals, 7, 9, 10, 11, 20, 22, 23, 27, 30, 31, 38, 43, 44, 46, 47, 50, 56, 58, 64, 68, 69, 75, 76, 86, 93, 95, 98, 103, 105, 110
seasons in the Arctic, 7
Sedna, 8, 17, 68–69, 70–72, 73, 74–75, 76, 77

shamans, 10, 13, 17, 40, 68–69
shelter, 10–11
Siberia, 6
singing duels, 14
Snow Bunting, 17, 60, 62, 64
snow houses. *See* igloos.
souls, 9, 75, 76, 80, 81, 89, 90
South America, 6
Spencer, Robert F., 66
spirit helpers and protectors, 17, 18, 57, 60, 62, 64, 66, 81, 91
spirits, 9, 10, 25, 57, 69, 72, 73, 75, 76, 77
stone houses, 10, 23, 56, 62
storytellers, 13–14, 25
sun, 6, 8, 22

T

taboos, 9, 68
Taku, 97–98, 100, 101–102, 103, 104
transportation, 11
Tuku, 28, 29-30, 38
tundra, 7, 18, 44, 56, 57, 81, 90, 95, 97, 98, 100
Tunrit, 56

U

umiaks, 11, 43–44, 46, 48, 49, 80, 89
Unangan Island, 15

W

walruses, 7, 11, 20, 22, 68, 75, 76, 86, 95, 98
whales, 7, 11, 20, 22, 68, 75, 76, 79, 95, 107, 109, 110, 111, 112, 116
witches, 17, 18, 57, 59–60, 62, 64
wolves, 57, 62, 63, 79

Y

Yupik, 13, 16